I0394351

Greetings From LA: 24 Frames and 50 Years

Second Edition

Greetings From LA: 24 Frames and 50 Years

Second Edition

A solo exhibition of new photographic collage works
by George Porcari at haphazard.

January 9–February 20, 2016

Second Edition
The first edition was printed in 2016 and coincided with an
exhibit at haphazard gallery. It featured an edited version
of the essay "Photographic Adventures with Edgard Degas"
and an essay not found in the second edition titled
"Gone to Hollywood: Annie Leibovitz and Helmut Newton
Shoot the Stars." The second edition contains "The Delight
of the Particular: The Photography of Ronald Traeger" by
George Porcari and "El Laberinto Dos" by Mark Von Schlegell
not found in the first edition.

DELANCEY STREET PRESS
1133 Venice Blv., Los Angeles, CA 90015
www.delanceystreetpress.com

Copyright © George Porcari, 2016
All photographs copyright the artist.

All rights reserved. No part of this book shall be
reproduced, stored in a retrieval system, or
transmitted by any means—electronic, mechanical,
photocopying, recording, or otherwise—without
written permission from the artist.

Designed by Karen Davison

Cover: GFLA Venice 1979

ISBN: 978-0-578-53866-2

23456789

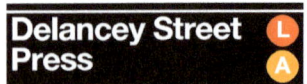

Greetings From LA

24 Frames and 50 Years

Second Edition

George Porcari

"I write: I inhabit my sheet of paper, I invest it, I travel across it.

I incite *blanks*, *spaces* (jumps in the meaning: discontinuities, transitions, changes of key).

I start a new paragraph. I refer to a footnote.[1]

I go to a new sheet of paper."

I write in the margin

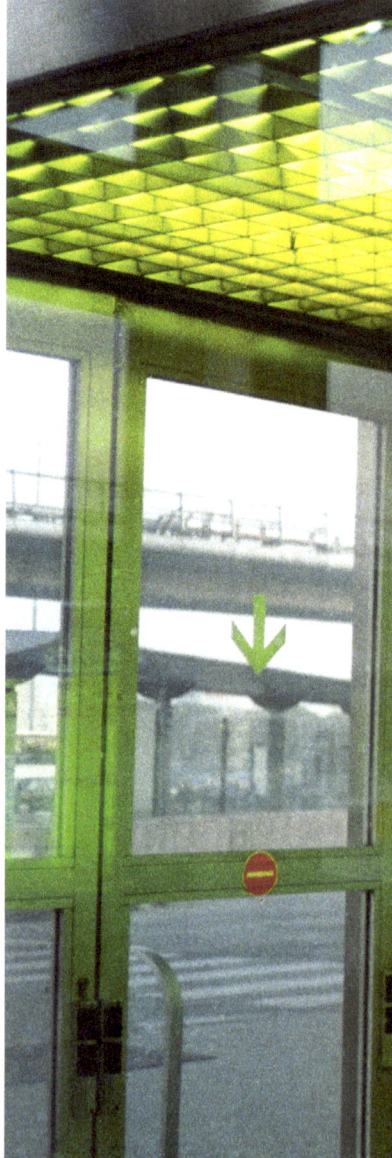

1984 A Traveler (for Chris Marker)

---

1   I am very fond of footnotes at the bottom of the page, even if I don't have anything in particular to clarify there.

—Georges Perec

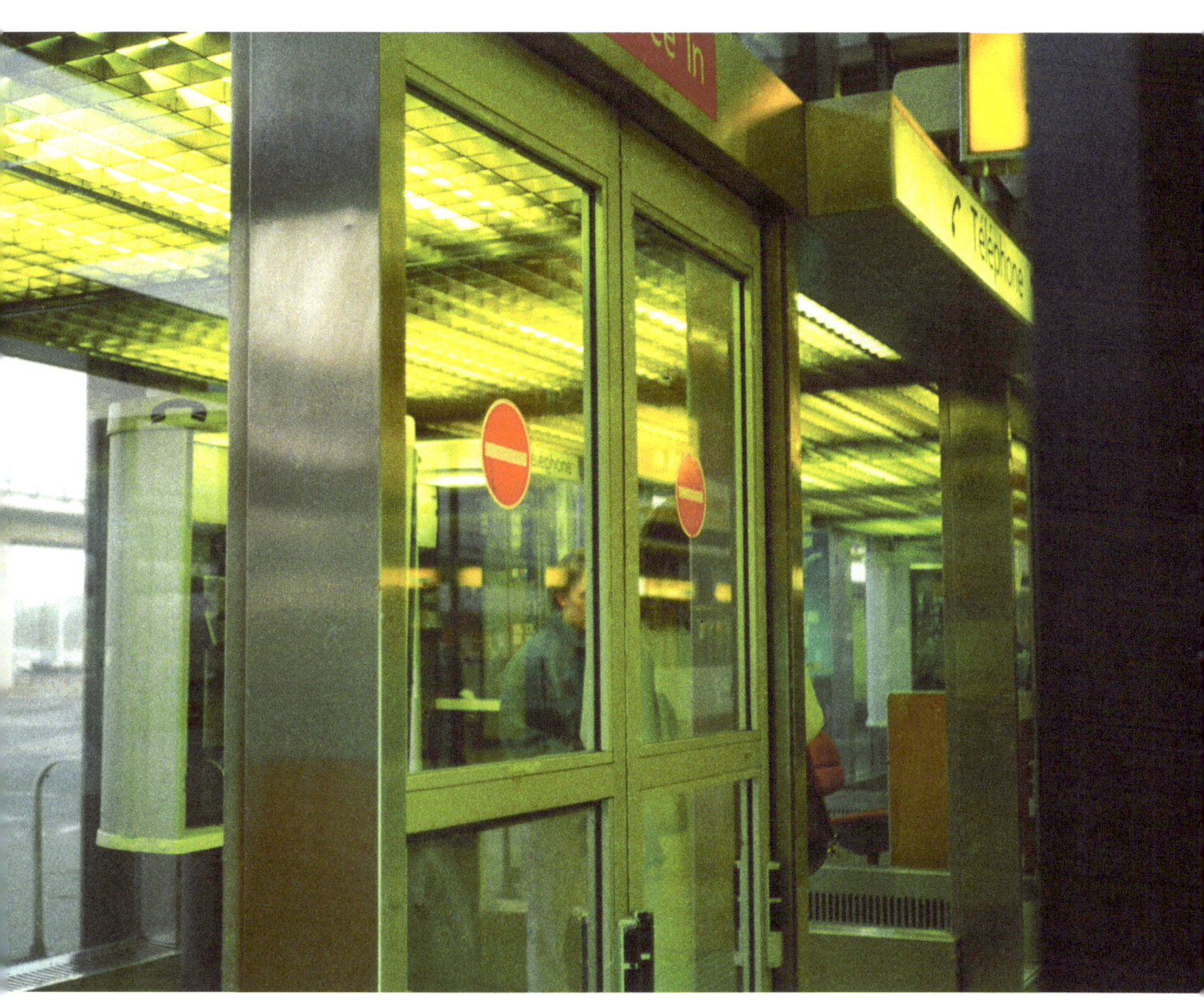

Table of Contents

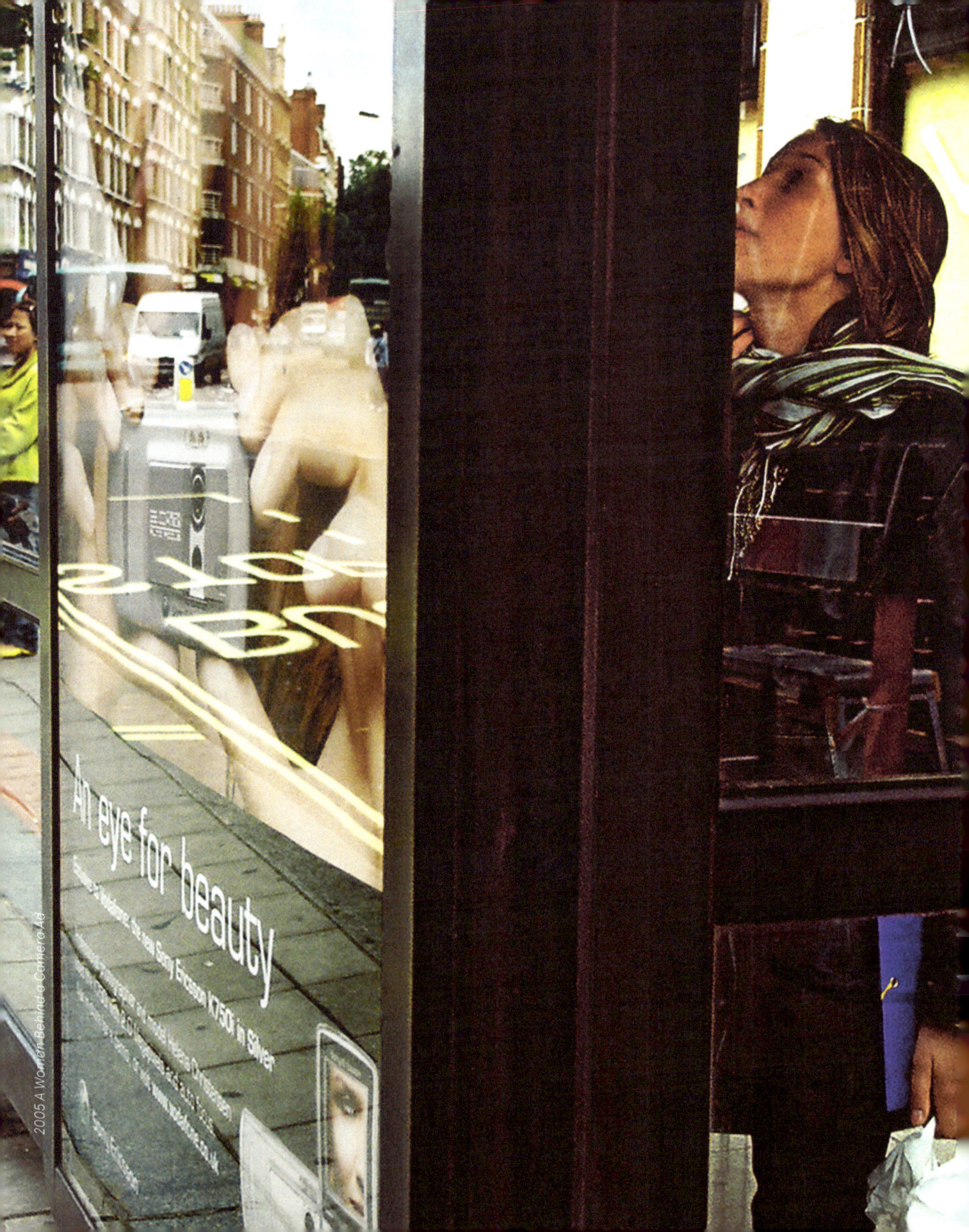

2005 A Woman Behind a Camera Ad

An eye for beauty

Introduction

Jorge Pardo

The following quotations are from Walter Benjamin:

The creative in photography is its capitulation to fashion. 'The World Is Beautiful'—this, precisely, is its motto. In it is unmasked the posture of a photography that can endow any soup can with cosmic significance but cannot grasp a single one of the human connections in which it exists... [1]

What, in the end makes advertisements superior to criticism? Not what the moving red neon says—but the fiery pool reflecting it in the asphalt? [2]

The camera introduces us to unconscious optics as does psychoanalysis to unconscious impulses. [3]

In times of terror, when everyone will be something of a conspirator, everyone will be in a situation where he has to play detective. [4]

The illiterate of the future will not be the man who cannot read the alphabet, but the one who cannot take a photograph. [5]

Not for nothing were the pictures of Atget compared with those of the scene of a crime. But is not every spot of our cities the scene of a crime? Every passerby a perpetrator? Does not the photographer—descendant of alchemists and mediums—uncover guilt in his pictures? [6]

—Walter Benjamin

George makes funny pictures...always off... blurry or framed in the wrong way...framed where normal productiveness makes no sense...falls apart...aspiring to painting slightly... rooted in documentation but never satisfying the event!...I can never use a convention with it so I have to be the producer of that document...it doesn't give me those ready-made conventions of snapshots, journalism or art photography that I can use as a tag...without the tag people get antsy or outright belligerent...obsessed with the photographs normal people would never show to others...like accidental images...

I once told George that his pictures made it seem like his camera had fallen out a window while driving and taken some pictures when it hit the pavement!...white noise was a term used then...the picture most people see nothing in...

yet still literalized as perfectly adequate documents representing the places where they were made...sort of...there is a very special awkwardness in the pictures...takes a little time...a little discernment to decide or inscribe what they are...hopelessly open...unsatisfying moments in the world not many like to be in... I like being there...this all seems to link nicely with a comment George always likes to make... I want to take pictures of nothing...taking pictures of nothing can only be done when the photographer is slippery, disheveled, optically un-rooted, undercover or pretty much trying to hide...eavesdropping and sneaking up on people...I have said to George..."remember George, people who go around taking pictures of nothing are always hiding shit"...best...jp

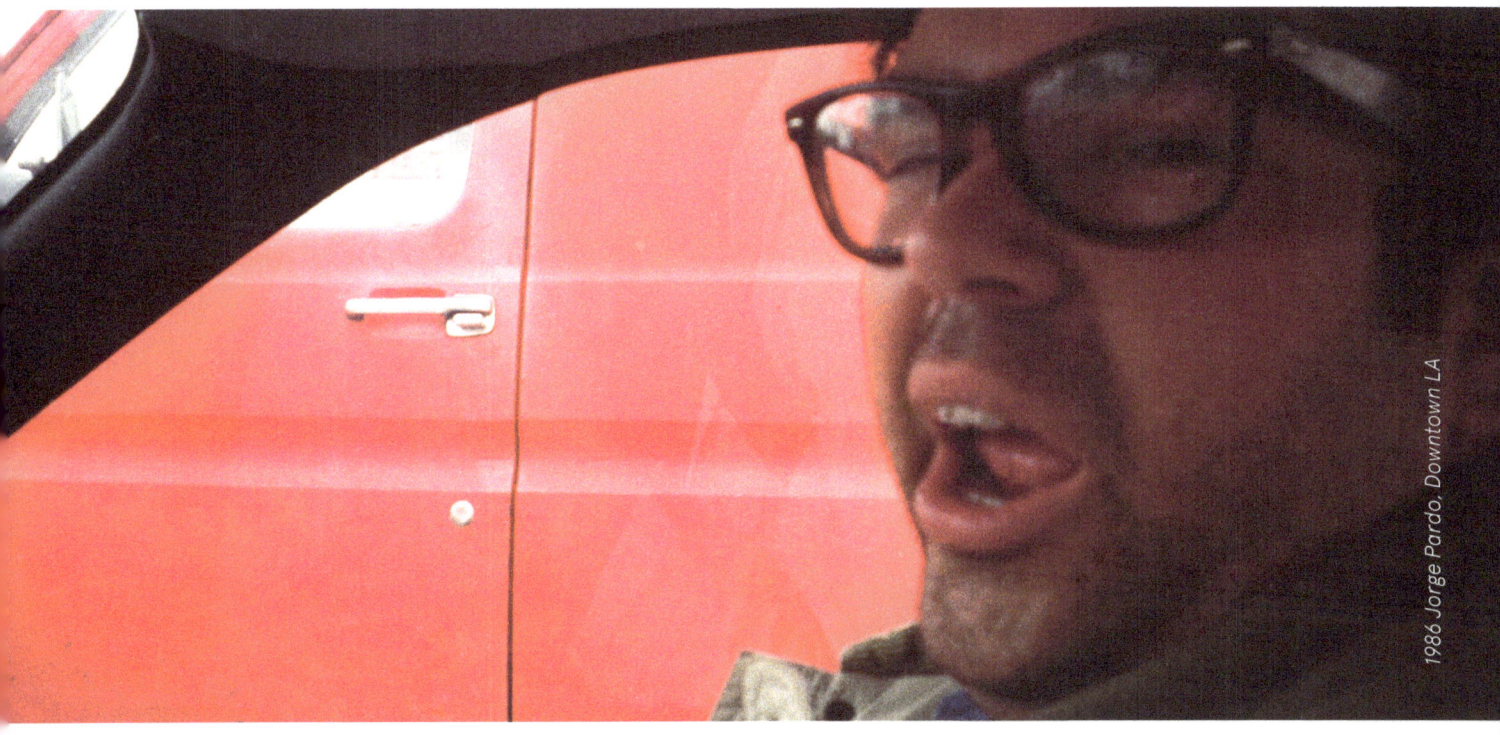

1986 Jorge Pardo, Downtown LA

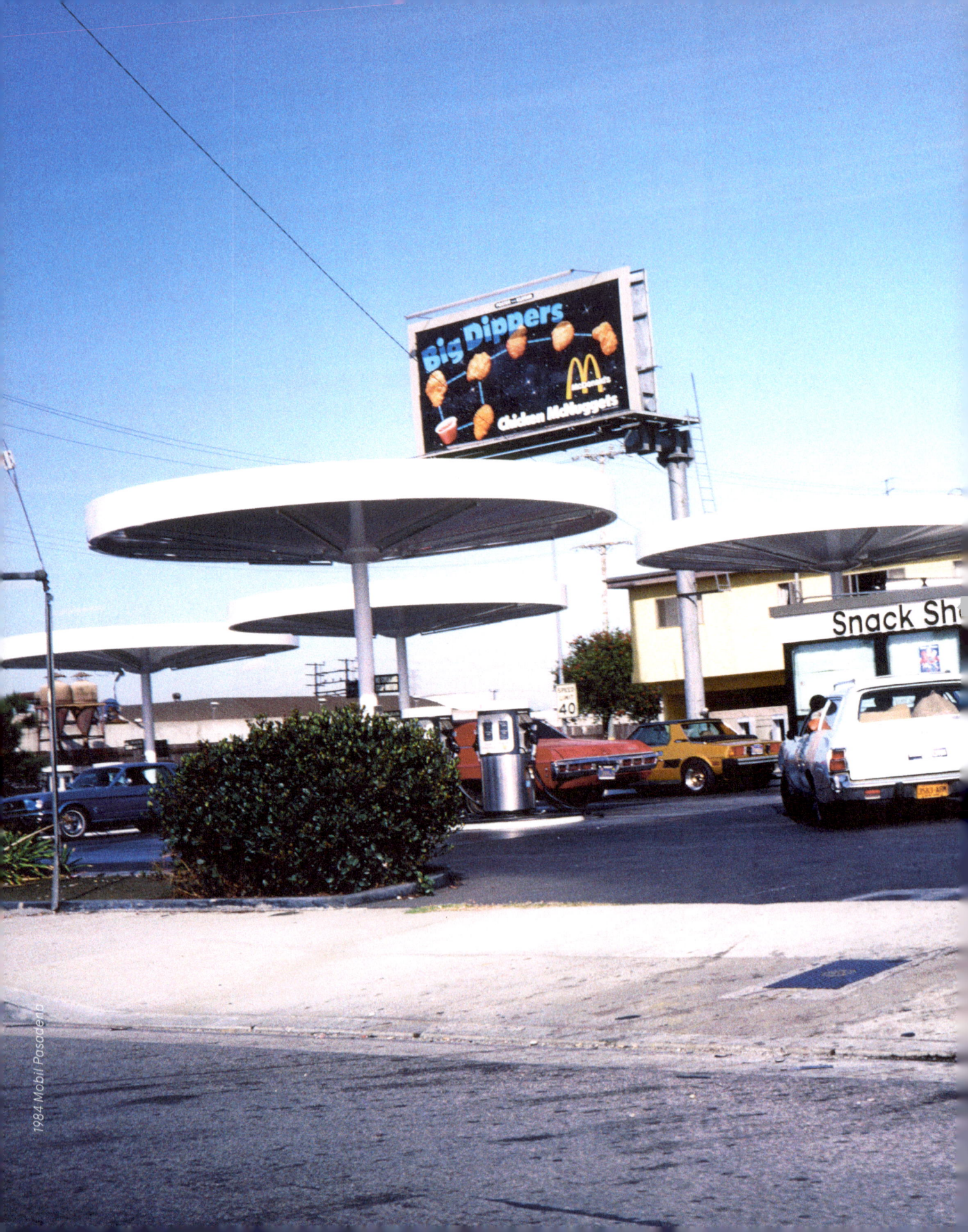

1984 Mobil Pasadena

Shooting Nothing in LA

George Porcari

There was in the 1980s a populist joke about Seinfeld: it's a show about nothing. While this statement is far more complicated than it first appears, it is in effect criticizing Seinfeld for not enacting conventional dramatic (or melodramatic) narrative tropes—with the exception of the final episode they were thankfully absent from Larry David and Jerry Seinfeld's brilliant episodic non-narratives.

What I've sought to do with pictures from early on—for me that is the seventies—was to be a photojournalist but one devoted to nothing. Photojournalism by its very reason-for-being seeks out the dramatic (or the melodramatic) and exposes it, dramatizes it, illustrates it, or explores it—depending on the temperament of the photographer. I consciously sought out non-moments, but ones familiar to me from everyday life as I knew it.

This proved far more difficult than I could have imagined—for what I came away with was often less than nothing—mere illustration of banality or, worse, abstracted spaces that were artful. At best they resembled Garry Wynogrand's more off kilter color work—a photographer I much admire—but Los Angeles in the seventies was such a peculiar place that it seemed to require something more or something else— but what was it?

Cut to New York City 1979. I got a job at the Strand bookstore on 12th and Broadway and a studio on the Lower East Side on Delancey St. near the Williamsbourg Bridge. The apartment was on the third floor but faced the bridge so it seemed as if it was on street level. I photographed this odd view only once with that peculiar kind of biting cold you get in the city that shows through somehow. You can see the projects on the south side of Delancey with a strange pair of trousers hanging off a window doomed to never get dry.

That year I took a picture of Canal Street near West Broadway (Canal St., 1979) that had what I had been searching for—the non-moment had transformed itself into magic. That picture kept my hopes alive that I could make pictures using a camera. Later I realized that that photograph owed a lot to Saul Leiter's work—who was then also living in New York, but unfortunately I didn't discover his photography until many years later, when the book on his early color work was published. If I had been aware of it

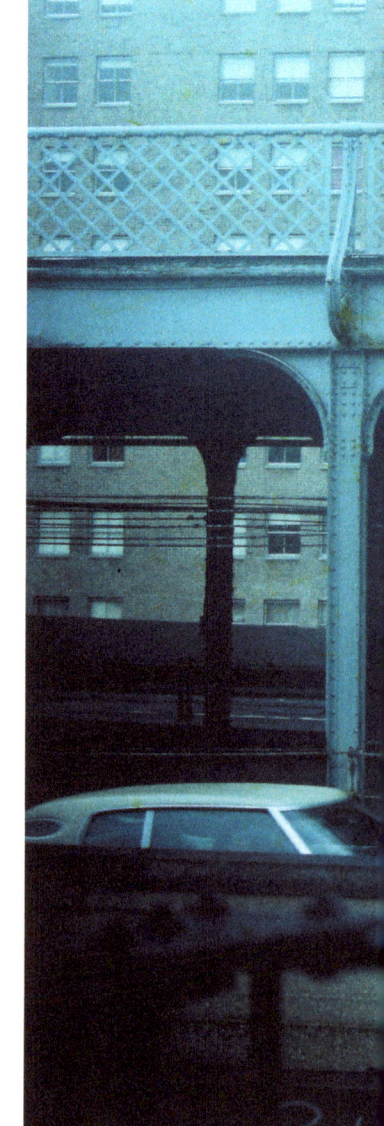

1980 View from My Window (Williamsbourg Bridge)

14

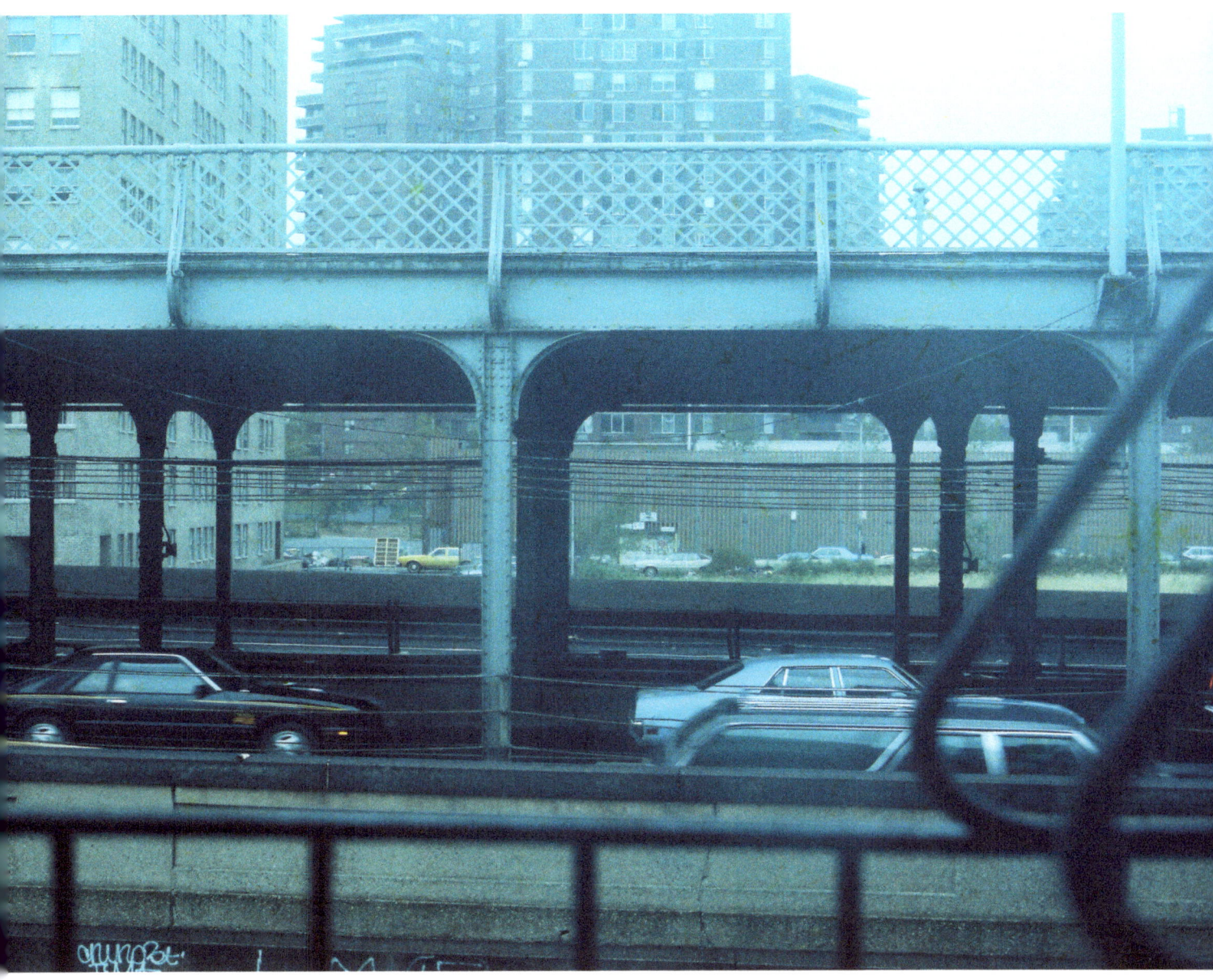

he might have saved me countless years of experimentation! As it was New York itself was my university—and all other schooling I did before or after was merely window dressing where I made some wonderful friends.

The 24 collages that constitute the *Greetings From LA* series come after many different experiments with collage starting in the 1980s. In that era of post-modernisms and Seinfeld I sought to make long strips using my own pictures and appropriated images together in long rows—in effect making storyboards for films that had gone off kilter and the various narrative lines ended up going nowhere, or into some mad metanarrative.

All the clues were false clues. All of the roads simply led to other roads. The emotional tone varied, often within the work, and this I think confused the few that saw the work—but they were a great deal of fun to make. Meanwhile I took full advantage of the strip format, taking the same liberties as filmmakers, and made adaptations of famous works including *Death in Venice* (as one example mentioned by Veronica Gonzalez in her essay) but transformed the ending into the highly implausible one of a friend's dog enjoying a sunny day on the beach in LA.

In the seventies, when I was a fanatic for films, I often went to projections in Los Angeles at the Cinematheque 16 in Pasadena, and the New Vagabond in McArthur Park, and later in New York in various places downtown that showed films I wanted desperately to see—from Andy Warhol's *Chelsea Girls* at a loft in Soho where you had to bring some chips or cheese to get in, to Godard's *Made in USA* (then unavailable) at the Mudd Club.

The films shown were not always classic films—at times they were simply travel images, pornography of sorts, formalist exercises still fresh from graduate school or found footage that had been spliced together in some random order—or at times the order was very carefully articulated, but only appeared random, and there would be a mimeographed sheet explaining the film—sometimes quoting from philosophers or academics.

If there were any chairs in such screenings they were usually the metal folding sort but I was in my twenties and spending several hours in the same position on a metal chair was a cakewalk. The 16mm and Super-8 projections often encountered a flicker effect when the projector jammed slightly—sometimes if it got serious the film would burn and have to be

"Today I touch my chin in retreat and in these momentary trousers I tell myself: So much life and never! So many years and always my weeks!"

—Cesar Vallejo

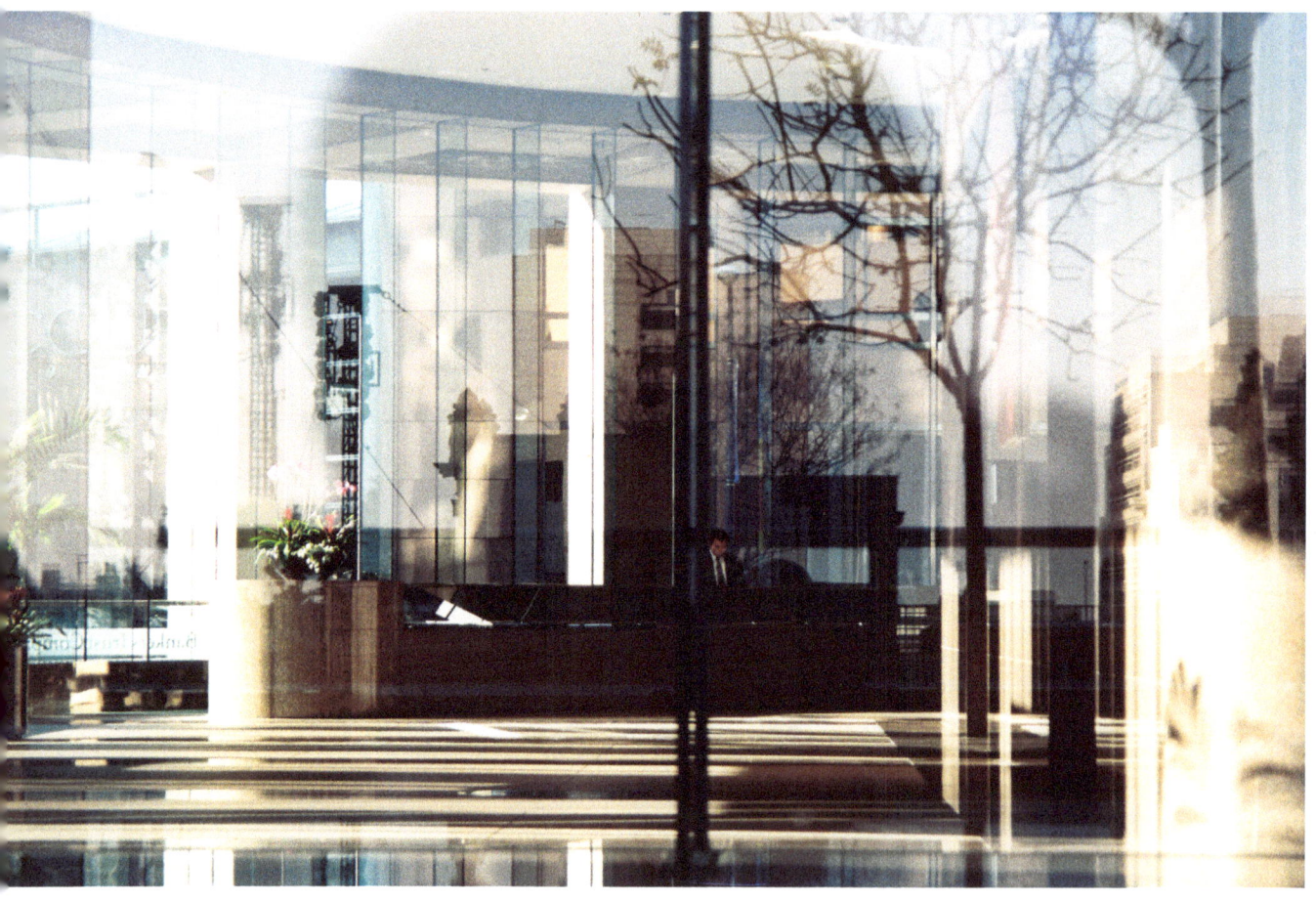

2001 Guide To LA (for Joan Didion)

re-threaded through the machine. These flickers where the film stopped for one second and vibrated on screen were often quite beautiful—in fact such was the variety and quality of avant-garde cinema that sometimes they were the highlight of the evening. Those flickers have stayed with me longer than many of the films seen then, much as I appreciated the time and work that went into their making.

In the current series *Greetings From LA* as well as the previous series, *Insistent Particularities*, that flicker finally gets the homage that it deserves. While the collages are also the result of years of making posters, for Rockypoint Press and Semiotext(e), the origins of it are in those wonderful screenings where I learned so much. While the two images are the same they are also different—the cropping and color correction are sometimes night and day.

The empty paper in between of course is not really empty—it's a meditative event of sorts where two images, from the same source, multiply and split off, its bottom partner still under the pressures of compression—as if it had been forced through a filament, which in effect it has. That empty space is as much a representation, or a field of play as the images.

The paper is also the support, for photographs have used paper since William Henry Fox Talbot's days and his famous "pencil of nature" but now it's an inkjet print. The images themselves cover the last fifty years of photographs that I've done in my hometown, Los Angeles.

Those 24 frames—or one second in film time—have also compressed fifty years. That stretching and pulling of time is something you get to understand quite well—with time. I wasn't born in LA but came from somewhere else (Lima, Peru in my case) like so many transplants to California and have stayed on, for no real or logical reason (none that could be made into a drama and certainly not a melodrama)—but after so many years that photojournalism of nothing I've been doing seems to have finally found a home.

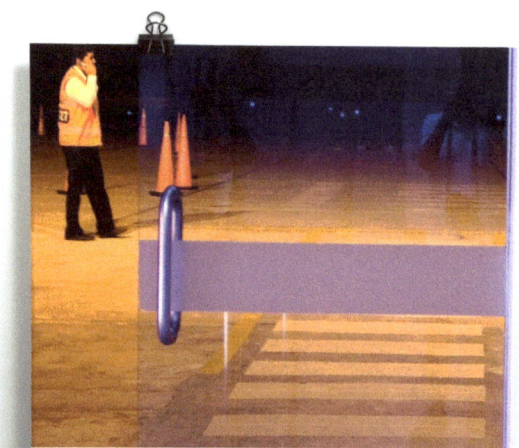
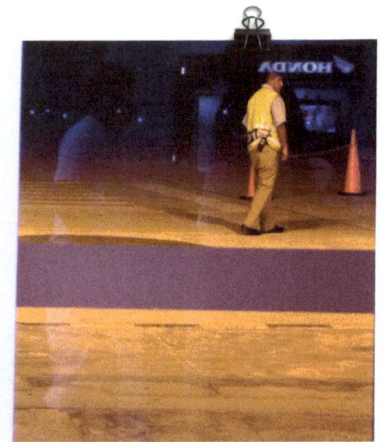

Insistent Particularities, an exhibition at Tif's Desk, Los Angeles, October, 2012

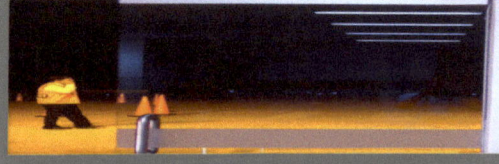
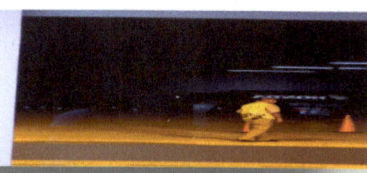

Insistent Particularities

Sylvère Lotringer

For a number of years, George Porcari resisted the comfort of his own medium. He made pictures or framed pictures, in such a way that they eschew narration, representation and signification, any direct apprehension of their material. First he shot photographs through glass windows, telephone booths or revolving doors, reflective structures that made his subjects more opaque and fleeting, impermanent.

In this new series of 32 photographs, he now uses small fragments of photographs, snatches of everyday life barely recognizable, often repeated with some distortion in the same photograph as a way of framing what interests him most—the wide stretch of matte white paper that lays in between. Hovering between abstract painting and concrete poetry, Porcari brings out a representation that represents nothing else but its own effort to make its disappearance visible.

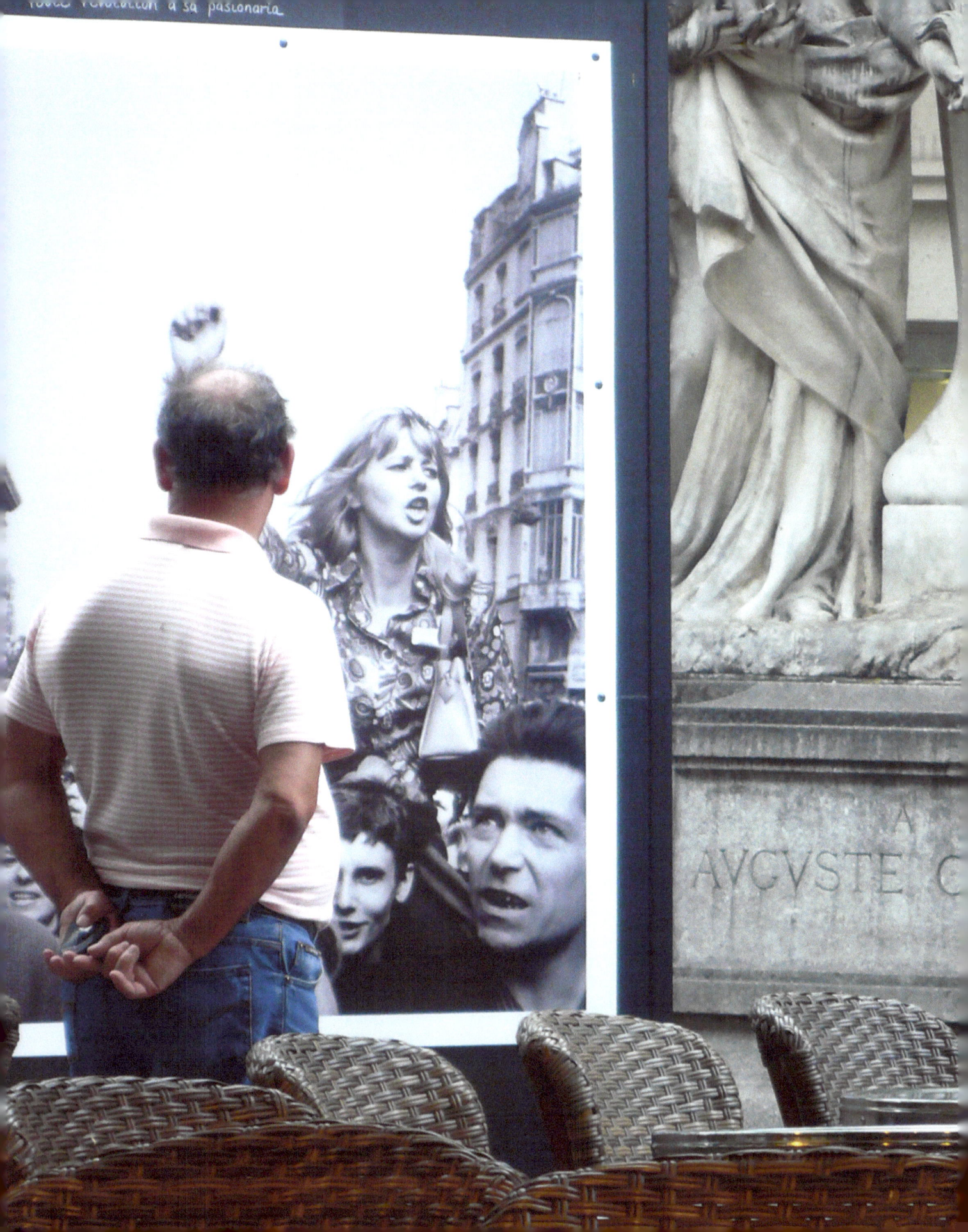

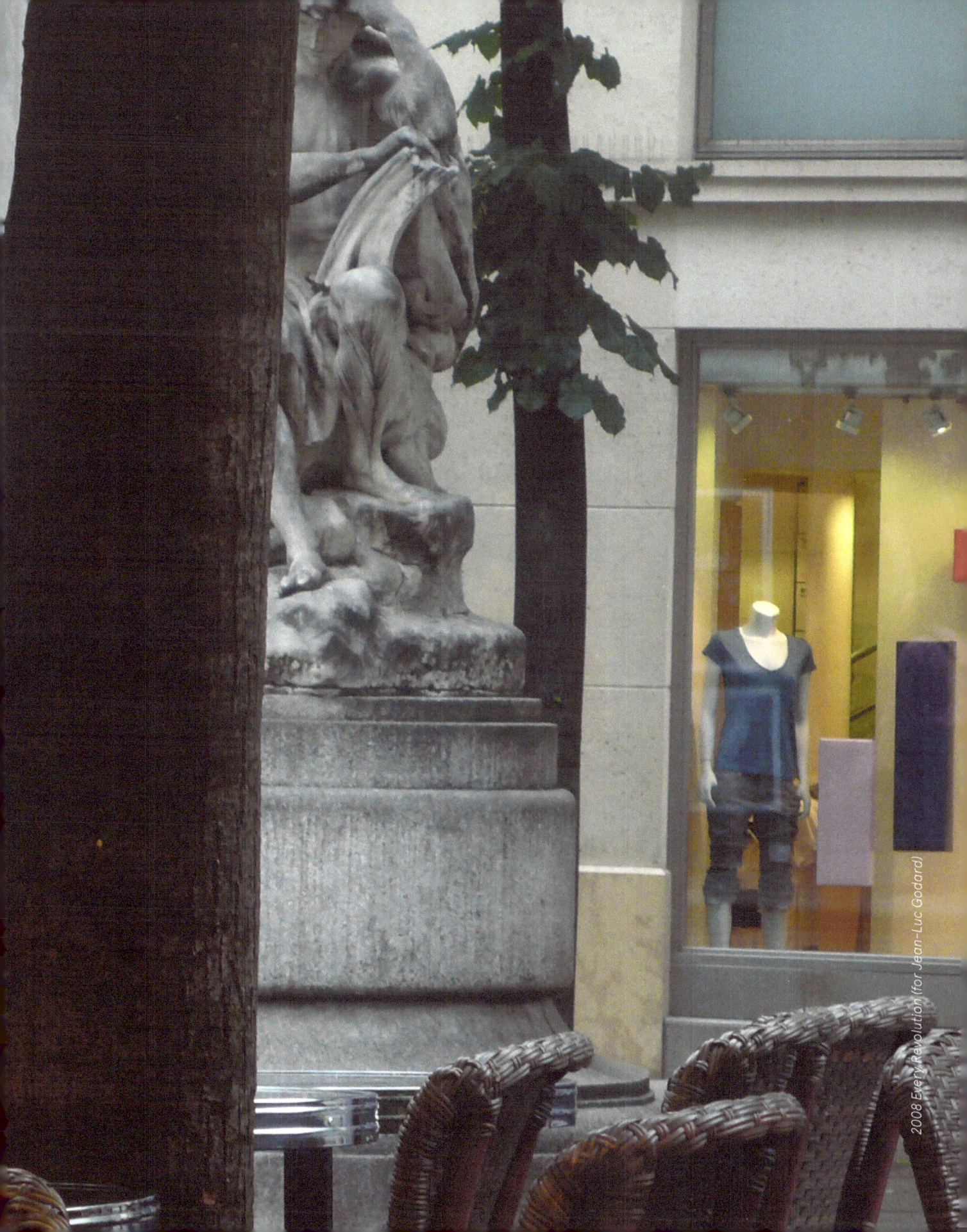

2008 Every Revolution (for Jean-Luc Godard)

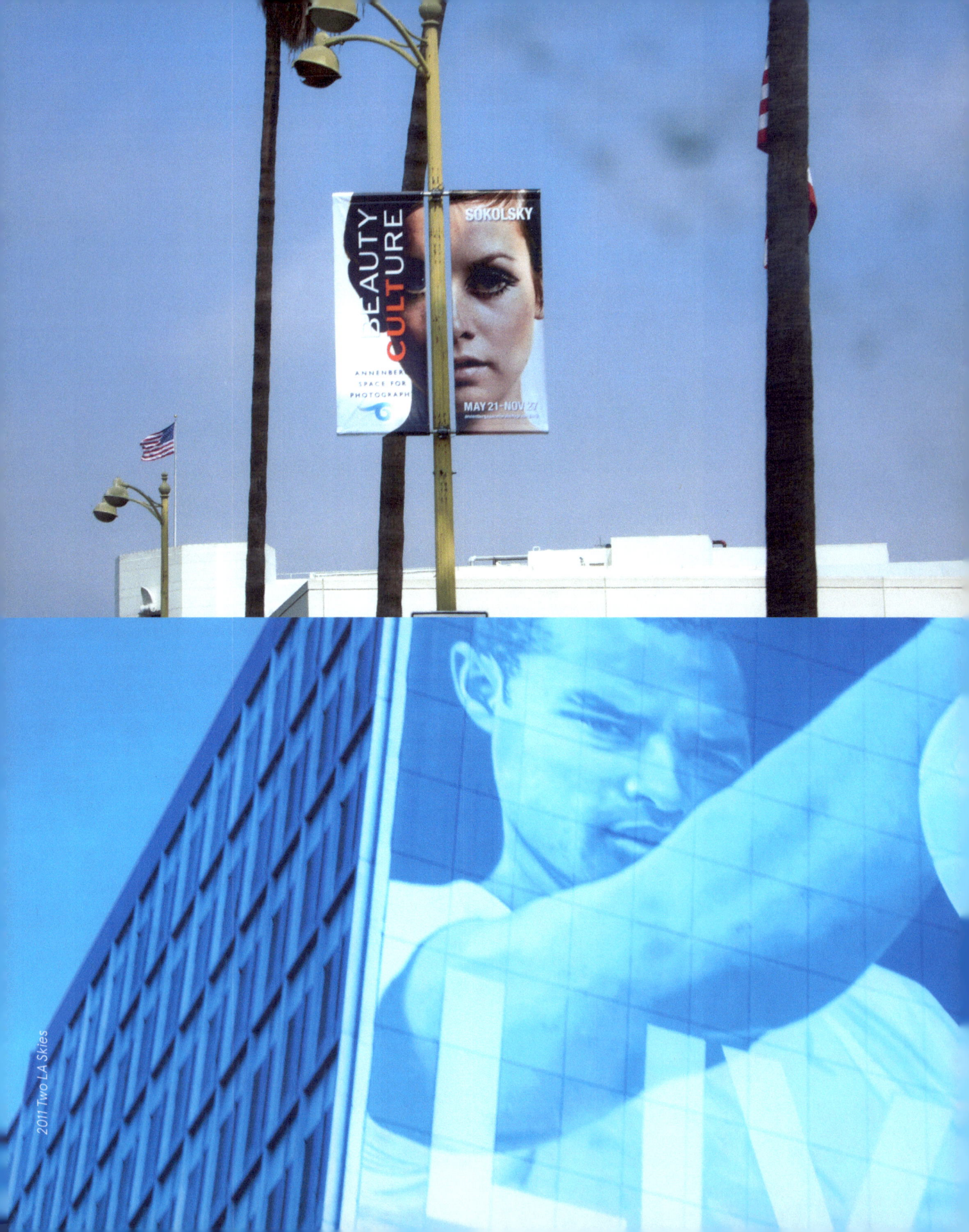

2011 Two LA Skies

Photographic Adventures with Edgar Degas

George Porcari

The photography of Edgar Degas, mostly in the form of duotone and tritone plates, was never exhibited in his lifetime, as these images first came to light, at least to the larger public, during a traveling exhibition in the late 1990s titled *Edgar Degas: Photography*. The photographs revealed a different Degas to the artist we thought we knew: From his mastery of the "master drawing" to his modernist framing; from his obsession with young dancers to his ability to find the right pose—both casual and classical at the same time—that could seemingly open up the world of the 19th century to us as clearly and beautifully as Zola or Proust. *That* Degas we knew—perhaps too well—but there was another person that was revealed to us through his use of photography: A sarcastic, smart-ass, subversive critic, playing with images. The photographer Degas speaks eloquently about his own time, and ours too by default, and it is *that* Degas that is the subject of this essay.

In 1885, at the height of the popularity for academic art and neoclassical tableaus—when Venuses in contorted poses that signified

"Do not wait for the last judgment—it takes place every day."

—Albert Camus

"classical" were all the rage—Degas made a photograph and titled it *The Apotheosis of Degas*. This was a ferociously brilliant and acerbic re-creation of Jean-Auguste-Dominique Ingres' *The Apotheosis of Homer* (1827). Werner Hofmann calls the image "... a joke with several layers of meaning which were long overlooked because Degas hid them behind his ostensible admiration for Ingres... with this self-mockery, Degas opened up a new dimension for photography..."[1] The image is the first work of photographic criticism directly aimed at the art establishment of his time— what Degas termed "the art police."[2] The work is clearly satirical in a manner that we don't normally associate with Degas—it is maybe more in keeping with Toulouse Lautrec or Honoré Daumier who did go in for satire that was sometimes very obvious and blunt. More to the point, Degas' satire comes to us not as a painting, a lithograph or a drawing, but as a photograph, and it is neither blunt nor obvious—what is Degas up to?

Let's start with the subject of Degas' satire. Ingres' painting shows the great men of various centuries, such as Dante and Moliere, in heaven placing a crown of laurels on the balding head of Homer. The bodies in Ingres' work are perfectly sculpted idealized figures, which

would have surprised the family members of many of the assorted greats, as the physiques and gestures of the participants do not come from any reality regarding antiquity or the people portrayed. The everyday reality of the classical world is something that we can glimpse, if we are so inclined, in the writings of the historian Tacitus or the works of Petronius or Sappho—all writers who were there and eloquently describe what they experienced, each in their own way. What we have with Ingres' painting is fundamentally an illustration of 19th century academic conventions of how antiquity presumably looked—based partially on misunderstandings (the Hellenic Greeks and the Romans after them did not favor white unpainted marble) and partially on a romanticized Arcadia—a fantasy—that was, as we will see, politically as well as aesthetically motivated.

Neoclassicism's conventions started with a radical revolution about half a century before Ingres. In the "age of reason," Jacques-Louis David's paintings staged a mythic heroism that caught the imagination of many critics, from Denis Diderot in his time to Michael Fried in ours. Yet, David's highly theatrical heroics and the mannered self-consciousness of Ingres— and then a little later the labored kitsch of

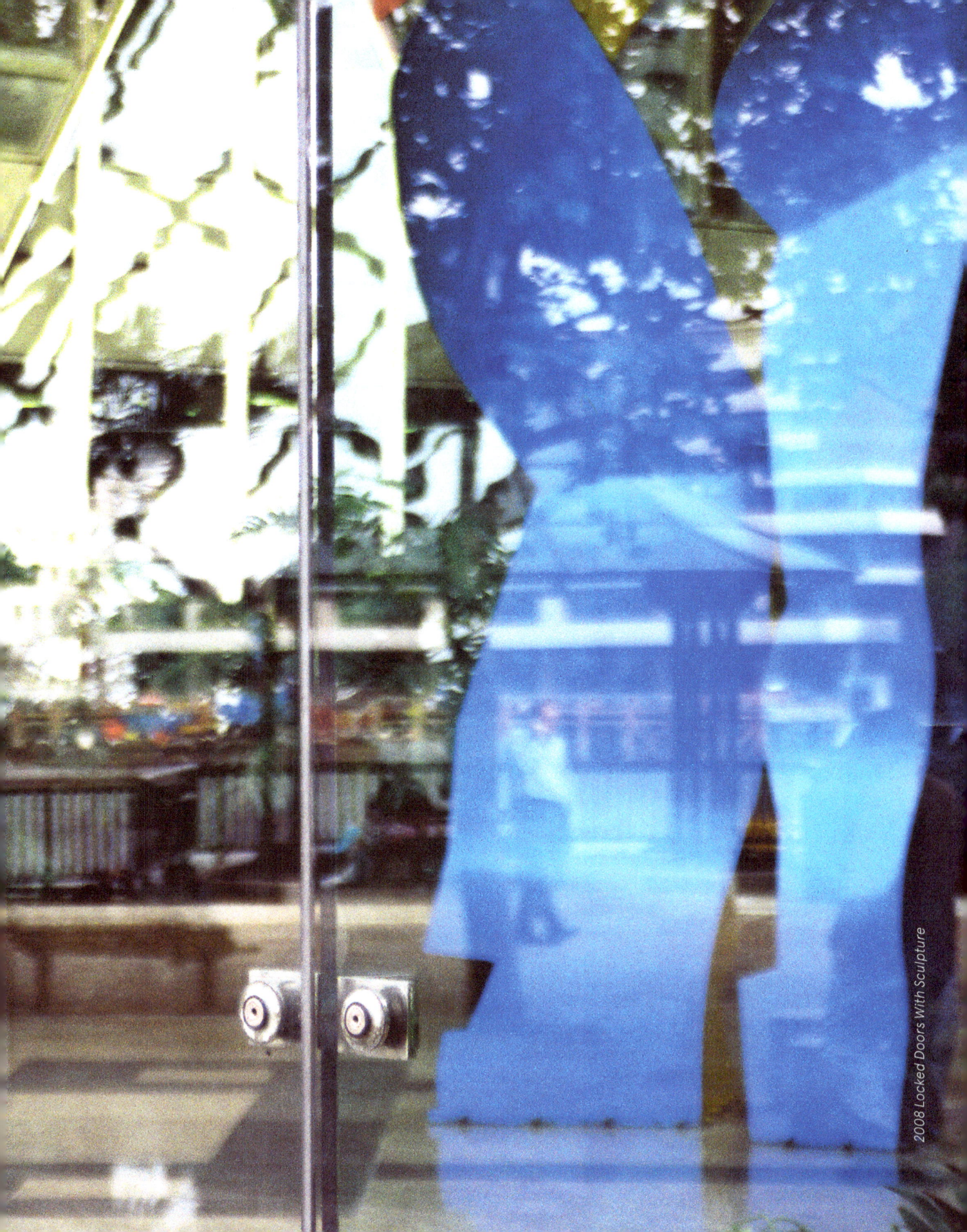

2008 Locked Doors With Sculpture

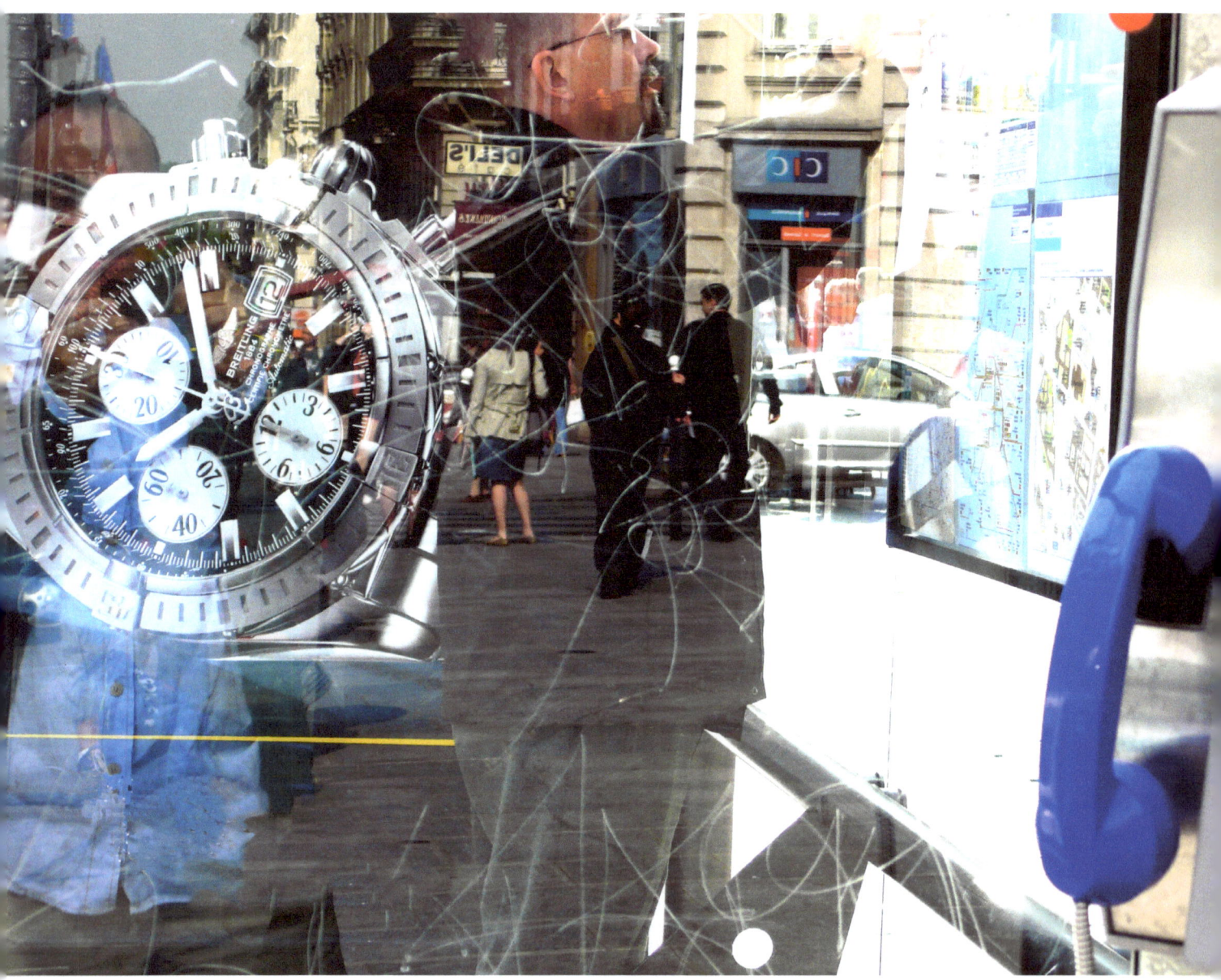

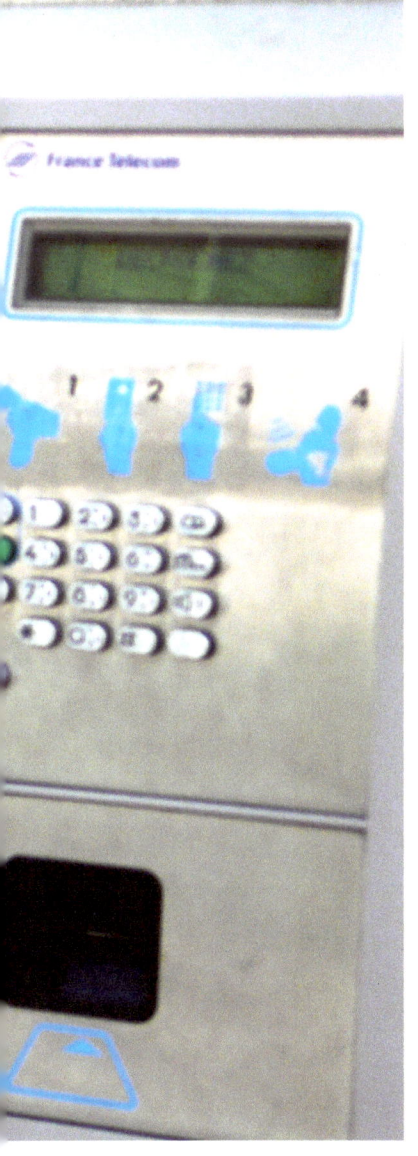

2008 Man Changing Bus Schedules

William-Adolphe Bouguereau—is but a short step of less than one hundred years. In Ingres' painting, all the hallmarks of neoclassicism are in place: The complex hierarchical order, the idealized harmony of opposites, an orchestration of differences with subtle narrative clues linked to classical literature, a high degree of conceptual rigor in the deployment of symbolism, and, perhaps most important of all, easily read emotional cues that favored heroism, traditional values and sentimentality.

That the state would favor such an aesthetic system is borne out by the fact that the French government supported the artists, and institutions, that favored neoclassicism from 1789 to the early 20th century, when that aesthetic system collapsed due to the emergence of the new technological/electronic age and the catastrophe of WWI. Nevertheless, that is several generations of support for a system that the state perceived as fundamental to how viewers perceived the past and the present as it manifested itself in various representations in books and paintings, therefore we can assume that this idealized image was integral to the presentation and preservation of the state. It is no coincidence that Ingres' painting was meant to hang in one of the ceilings of the Louvre.

"I remember having experienced a great feeling of calm on reading Hegel in the impersonal framework of the Bibliotheque Nationale in August 1940. But once I got into the street again, into my life, out of the system, beneath a real sky, the system was no longer of any use to me: what it had offered me, under a show of the infinite, was the consolations of death; and I again wanted to live in the midst of living men."

—**Simone de Beauvior**, *The Ethics of Ambiguity*

As is to be expected, Ingres' vision of heaven favors the Roman Imperial style of architecture. The painting is based on Raphael's *Parnassus* (1511), a wall mural decorating one of the palaces in the Vatican. Raphael's ambitious fresco depicts a heaven-like Parnassus (a center of poetic or artistic activity) inhabited by famous cultural figures from the past, both mythic (9 muses) and real (Homer), in a theater-like setting.

In Ingres' *Apotheosis*, a word that means "to turn into a God," Raphael himself stands on the far left, hand to his heart, signifying in the language of academic painting his earnestness as he is experiencing some profound emotion. Everyone, including King Charles X who commissioned the painting, appears to be in deep thought, posing for an "official picture."

Charles X would be deposed in 1830, three years after the painting's completion, not because of Ingres' work, but through ineptitude and the mishandling of finances due to colonial misadventures, the most expensive and deadly being the conquest of Algeria as a French colony—a prize that the French would be hard pressed to surrender—the Algerians won back their independence only in 1962, after another brutal, drawn out war.

In the summer of 1885, Degas was staying in Dieppe with his childhood friend, Ludovic Halevy, and his family. The artist had depicted Ludovic a number of times over the years, most spectacularly in his brilliant *Place de la Concorde,* where we see Halevy and his two daughters crossing the nearly empty square. This is one of the first paintings to consciously use the off-center framing with subjects cut off at oblique angles by the frame—all qualities that were ascribed to photography's snapshot aesthetic. In the artist's black and white photograph, children place some branches from nearby trees near Degas' head of white hair. *The Apotheosis of Degas* was art directed by Degas, but was actually taken by Walter Barnes, a protégé of Degas. Three women (the fact that there are three would make them muses in the language of neoclassicism that Degas is satirizing) hold branches, standing over the seated Degas, while two boys half-kneel by his feet. In 1885, the artist was sixty, but he looks much older and worn out, melancholic, impenetrable, and lost in thought. He is posing with his hat upside down between his legs as if it were a basin.

Degas helpfully performed a critique of his own photograph in a letter to Halevy: "My three muses and my choir boys should have been grouped against a white or pale background, the costumes of the women in particular are lost. And the figures should also have been closer together."[3] Degas' criticism is formally sound, but he does not point out any of the great subtleties in the picture. The upside-down hat between the artist's legs creates an ellipse that mirrors the crown of laurels above his head, creating a visual relationship that is funny as the bowler hat—a sign for bourgeois respectability—becomes a toilet. Degas is, in effect, satirizing the perfectly sculpted bodies in Ingres' painting by suggesting that such bodies are beyond the physical/animal act of producing shit—because they are not real. The ubiquitous bowler hat would become an ironic moniker of faux respectability in the coming century for artists like Magritte, and, later still, for Hans Richter in his wonderful surrealist film *Ghosts Before Breakfast* (1928). Degas seems to have intuited the whimsy in the bowler as a prop early on.

Degas' image is quietly revolutionary. It is the first break made by an artist using photography that visibly attacks the art conventions of his time—at least the first one that has survived. This is the first opening into how some people really felt about neoclassical art, but were not free to express because it went against social conventions and institutional norms within the bourgeois class. Not surprisingly, one catches glimpses of what people really felt in the popular illustrations of the time seen in newspapers and magazines, the caricatures, graffiti and popular songs of the period.

There is one very funny example from Honoré Daumier in *Charivati*—one of the most popular magazines of the time. Two women dressed in contemporary clothes—that is with many layers covering the whole body except for the face and hands—are in a salon showing paintings of naked women idealized to conform to the tastes of the period, and then placed in an Arcadian or classical landscape to italicize the nudity and put it within the context of "Art"— that is to transform them from naked to nude.[4]

One of the women in Daumier's drawing com-plains, while throwing her arms up in the air in disgust: "This year Venuses again...always Venuses!" Daumier's genius was clearly that he had a great ear to match his observant eye. The women know what art critics did not—that the "Venuses" were there for the titillation and amusement of the men, not because of their props or Arcadian setting—that only served to legitimize the nude. We see the same sorts of absurd bourgeois efforts in films and television

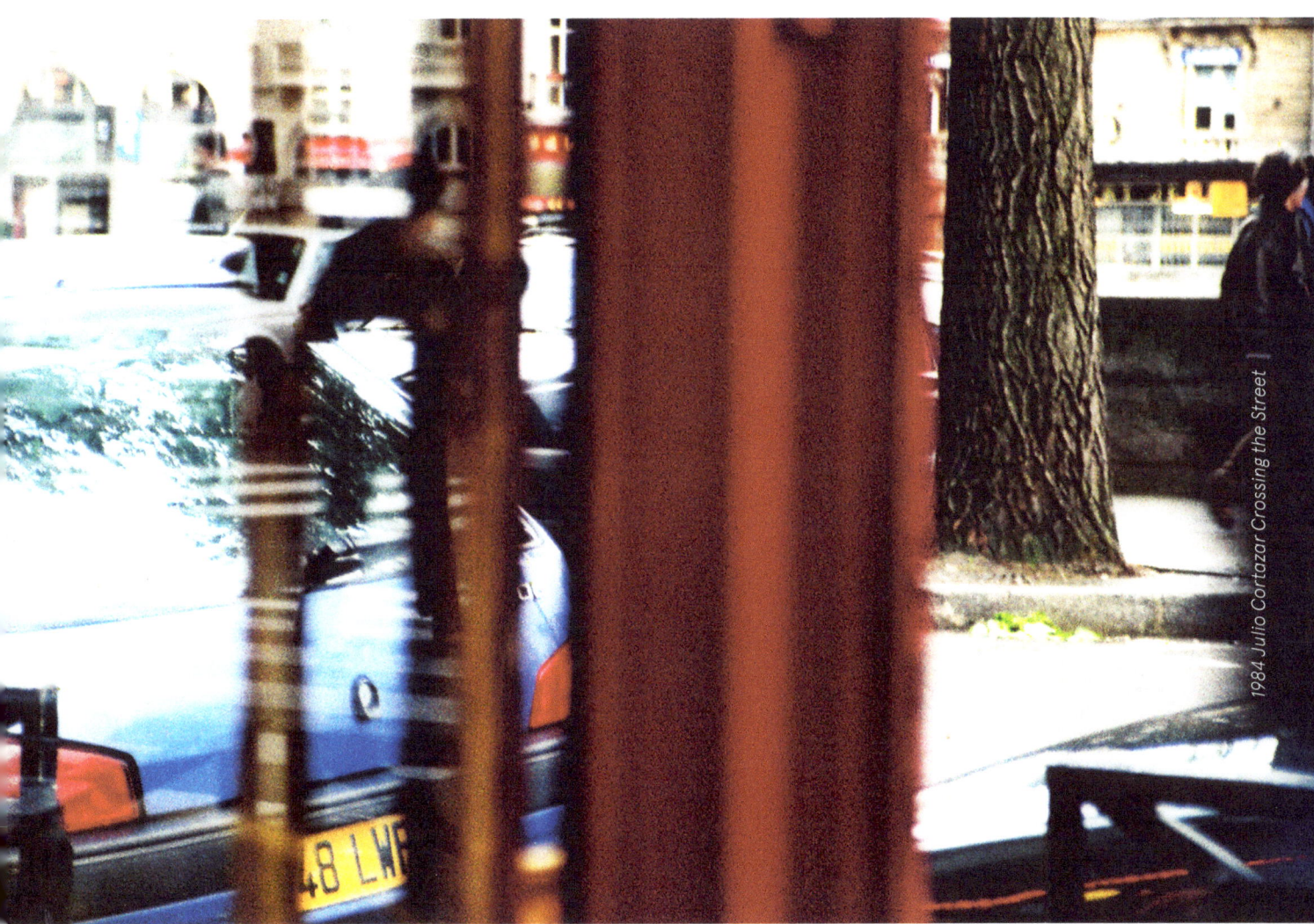

1984 Julio Cortazar Crossing the Street

"Degas is the perfect foil for his own satire."

today—to much the same sorts of wizened retorts from women who have seen it all. The popular drawings of the period tell us that Degas in his photograph was working within a well-established satirical tradition, but one that came from the bottom-up, that is, from the streets, the cafes, the laundry shops and the bars—not from the academies, the gentlemen clubs or the art salons. The Dadaists and Cubists would, a short time later (within Degas' lifetime), explore these conventions of realism and institutional norms at some length, and, in a sense, knock the doors off the hinges. But in 1885, no one ridiculed the ruling elite publicly, for to do so was suicide. Again, it is not so different today. Looking at this image is like seeing a whole century as if for the first time. It directly confronts the empty masks of the great men in Ingres' pantheon, and the emperor is not just naked, he's out of touch.

Ingres' fantasy heroics would, unfortunately, play themselves out in the following century, beginning with what was called "the war to end all wars" in 1914, as artists made advertising posters to promote patriotism and militarism using neoclassical motifs. The countries that participated in the many wars of the 20th century, large and small, might have hated each other's politics but they all loved neoclassicism

and used it to promote their military efforts. In terms of aesthetics, they all seem to have agreed that neoclassicism was the way to reach the masses emotionally and move them to accept undertakings that would probably not be in keeping with their self-interest. It would be interesting to know what the artists of this period would have thought of the use of neoclassicism to promote war on a massive industrial scale. Ingres never lived to see it; Degas did, but what he thought was not recorded.

We can see already in Degas' image the brilliant satires of the 20th century that were just around the corner, with the same sense of sarcasm and class consciousness. In Charlie Chaplin's *City Lights* (1931) the film begins with some pompous, overdressed politicians about to dedicate a heroic neoclassical tableau of life-size statues, but Chaplin has been sleeping on one of them (a woman with outstretched arms) because he's homeless. As he descends, its neighboring statue, sword in hand, skewers Chaplin by the seat of his pants, leaving him dangling and helpless.

In *Duck Soup* (1933), The Marx Brothers made fun of the herd instinct of American patriotism (and musicals), as Groucho Marx, the president of Freedonia, dances with a group of women performing a classical ballet. But the cigar in his hand and sarcastic expression totally undermine the classicism, and bring it crashing to the ground—even some of the ballet dancers had to laugh.

In both of these cases, classicism is having the rug pulled from under it—but Degas was there first. Unlike contemporary pastiche versions of neoclassical art, such as Bruce Nauman's *Self-Portrait as a Fountain* or Jeff Koons's *Llona's House Ejaculation*, Degas went much further and took greater risks. This is because Nauman and Koons have immediately placed their photographic work in quotes, making them Art as a matter of course. Degas' snapshot, homemade aesthetic keeps those quotes at a distance. It is, in some sense, a family picture—and as with any family picture, the primary risk is that you will look stupid and make a fool of yourself. Degas is the perfect foil for his own satire. The irony works on all fronts because he gives us an alternative vision to Ingres' massive painting that critics have missed, perhaps because it is too obvious. Put simply, this is a picture of people who loved each other and liked each other's company and wanted to make art together for the pleasure of it. They are the friends and children who

were as close as Degas, the shy bachelor, (one aspect of his complex personality) would ever get to having a family.

As a counter to Ingres' imperious twelve foot tall ceiling, it presents a small picture that you can hold in your hand. Ingres' work is about the presumed eternal power of certain classical conventions of visual presentation, and what Degas is suggesting as an alternative aesthetic is the snapshot. In effect, he uses his own intimacy with his friends, and the medium of photography, in an impromptu manner to talk about the distance between our mortal life here on earth and the heroic time-less ideals of Ingres' picture, or any aesthetic system such as neoclassicism—particularly its virulent 19th century model—that seek to explain reality by fitting it into a hierarchical system of knowledge that presumes to be beyond everyday life. This is why he needed photography. It couldn't be done as a drawing or a painting, as it wouldn't have the same emotional charge. What Degas was after was the love that you live out in the company of friends and family on a daily basis—a routine of love—something that cannot be extrapolated from a concept or theory; it must be physically experienced and improvised over time as a transitory experience.

This love, that is depicted in the snapshot, challenges death and oblivion, but does not reject it, as does neoclassical art that finds an escape clause in the contract; that is, a heaven, a place beyond the reach of transformation, decay and death. Ingres ingeniously conflates Bible illustrations with depictions of pagan classical antiquity that conform to contemporary (1827) tastes. That such a heaven, once it is "realistically" portrayed would be bound to historical details (such as the Roman architecture of the imperial period), is the crack in the foundation of neoclassicism from which the beautifully rendered edifice could never recover. Neoclassicism required a suspension of disbelief that was not tenable, once one understood the absurdity found in the details. Neoclassical art demands this suspension of disbelief—almost as an extension of religious belief itself—but, like religion, it cannot stand the scrutiny of historical investigation, nor an anthropological dissection of the details that make up the whole. Once the lights are turned on the masks, the sets and the costumes are revealed, and the illusion is shattered.

In this respect, it is helpful to keep in mind that what 19th century critics and collectors most despised about Impressionism (in some cases quite violently) was not its visible brushwork

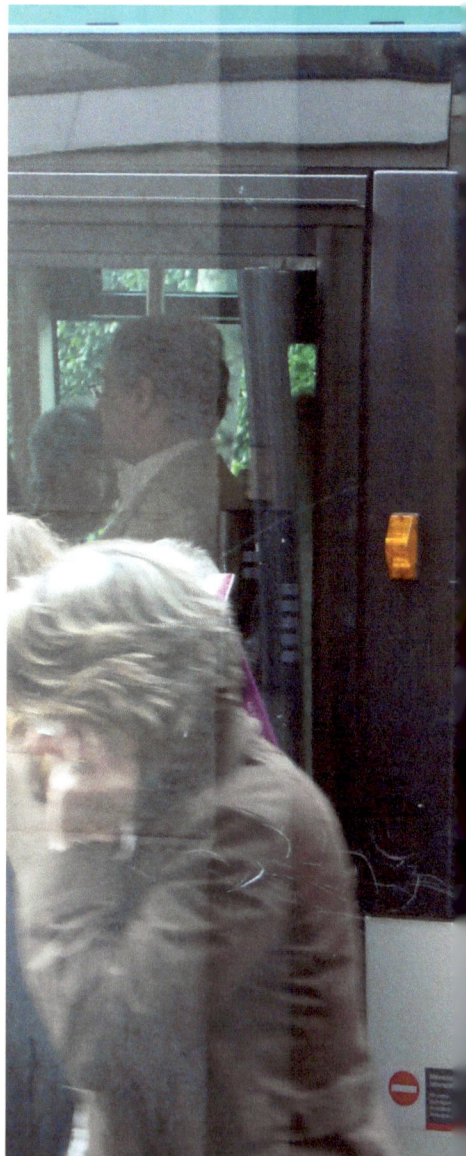

2008 France Bus Stop Crowd

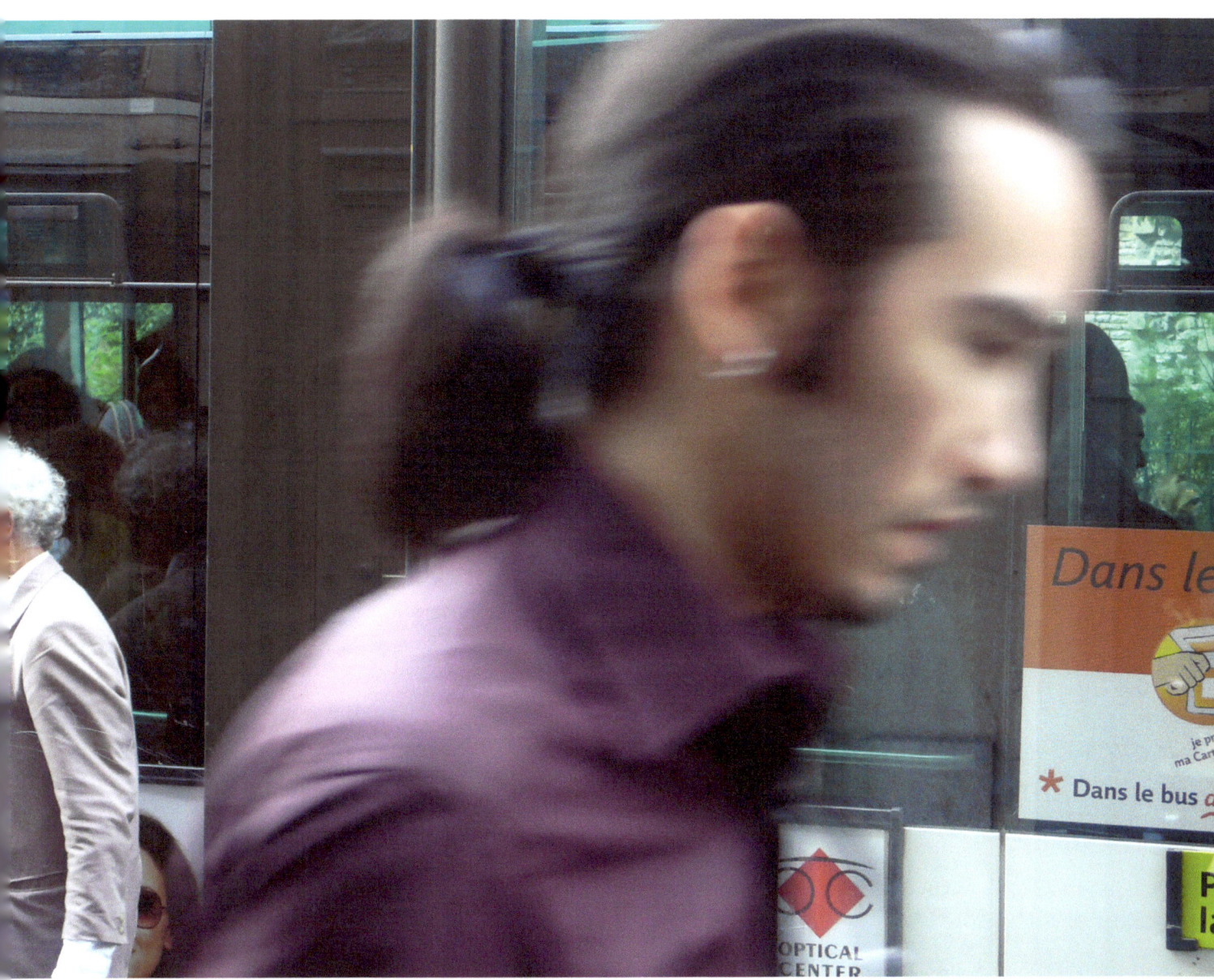

"Photography gets the transitory as no other tool has ever done..."

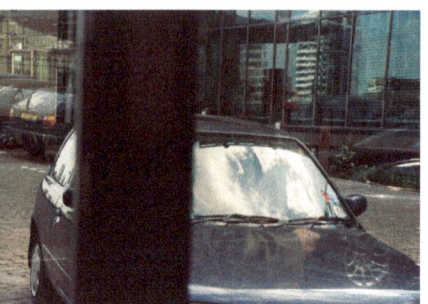

*2008 France Parked Car
With Clouds*

and bright palette, since these things had already been seen in the work of Gericault and Delacroix; nor the simple, quotidian subject matter that avoided heroics, since that had already been seen in the work of Corot and Millet. What they hated was the transitory aspect of the images, once Impressionists fixated not only on shifting patterns of light, but on evanescent quotidian moments that would shortly be gone forever. A wonderful example is provided by Claude Monet in *The Breakfast* (1868), a painting of Madame Monet enjoying breakfast while her workaholic husband seems to have pulled aside his chair and painted her before sitting down to enjoy his own.

Just as Monet beautifully mimicked the fugitive immediacy of the snapshot, some photographers were, conversely—or perversely—mimicking the effects and the motifs of neoclassicism through, often labored, technical manipulation in the darkroom. This group, who came to be known as Pictorialists, carefully followed the rigid program of composition laid out by neoclassical painting in order that their photographs might be considered art as a matter of course. Some photographers, like Gustave Le Gray, took landscape photographs that perfectly mirrored the conventions of framing and soft focus peculiar to painting. Ironically, Le Gray had to travel to the actual places that he photographed at great expense and physical danger—something that painters would have to submit to only if they wished it—a situation that ultimately bankrupted him. Others, like Oscar Rejlander or Henry Peach Robinson, took portraits that mimicked the effects of 19th century portrait painting—including Ingres—going so far as to create elaborate collages done in the darkroom from dozens of negatives exposed on the same piece of paper—dodging and burning to eliminate the seams and the formal effects of the collage.

The sentimentality, evident in Robinson's *Fading Away* (1858), comes to the forefront to create a facile illustration whose theatricality is referenced in the partially open curtains. The scene was, of course, staged for the camera over a period of time with not all of the actors being present in the room at the same time. The title of the work is meant to act as the trigger mechanism that allows the sentimental narrative free reign over the image so we may then successfully "read" all of the players and their stories correctly. The characters in Robinson's drama are unfortunately very quickly reduced to highly-organized and symbolic tableaux vivants, archetypes that

become merely a part of the symbolic order being illustrated, and it is this that becomes the central focus of the work rather than the individuality of the people involved, or the emotional content of the narrative. Unfortunately, archetypes, more often than not, reduce complex realities to the simplicity of an essence—a concept—that organizes the world for us and reduces it to a cliché.

Let's compare this image to Daumier's brutally realistic drawing *Flu Epidemic* (1858) that depicts a young family with a baby in a tram, the mother concerned and with a sense of tragic foreboding, the father lost in helpless reflection, and, most poignantly, the baby looking out at the world in sheer incomprehension, terror, and pain. The great photographer Felix Nadar suggested that in the future, people would find the drawings of Daumier impossible to believe because his realism would be mistaken for grotesque exaggeration.

In fact this is exactly what has happened. Daumier, in our time, is now taken to have been only a caricaturist prone to exaggeration for the sake of a laugh. Nadar, his contemporary, had a different opinion: Daumier "decisively cuts out these early effigies of bourgeois, janitors and bankers, creatures as strange as

Etruscans...(but) which coming generations will refuse to believe in, even though they are, alas!, and will remain, the perfect, daguerreotyped copy of real life in our "Belle-Epoque."[5] In Nadar's very modern use of quotation marks to signify an ironic overlay of meaning, one can already sense the biting sarcasm of "Belle-Epoque"—clearly asking, along with Daumier, belle for whom?

Photography gets the transitory as no other tool has ever done, and Degas not only got that aspect of it, but like any good modern artist, he worked with and against the grain of this strength by posing people (as Robinson did), but also emphasizing this as a single moment in time—in effect, he also got the transitory aspect. That he was familiar with the effects of photographic or snapshot framing is clear from his painting *Place de la Concorde* from a decade earlier than the satire of Ingres.

The snapshot aesthetics that Degas was experimenting with were then new and untested, and other contemporaries like Emile Zola, Jaques Henry Lartigue, Jacob Riis and Nadar experimented with photography (in very different ways), but unfortunately bad health and deteriorating eyesight limited Degas' future as a photographer. It is difficult to imagine what he might have achieved in this medium had he been able to take pictures until his final year (1917), but this photograph, taken with the help of his friends Walter Barnes, Ludovic Halevy and family, gives us a hint. Let's do a thought experiment and briefly imagine what Ingres might do if hired to illustrate love for an aristocrat's chateau.

One can see the winged cupid, the suggestive Venus gloriously naked in a pose borrowed from antiquity—or perhaps Botticelli's *Primavera*—the various arcane references to classical stories of love scattered across the canvas, the perfectly sculpted bodies going through the same tedious poses that would show off their torsos (and Ingres' rendering skill), the landscape in the background borrowed from one of Titian's erotic paintings, and the narrative lines deployed like a battle plan. Do we need to ask whose love this would represent? In Ingres, the clear idea always supersedes the messy reality.

The word apotheosis means to turn into a God, and Ingres, along with Charles X, no doubt had ambitions in that direction. Their ticket was a big painting that linked them to Homer via Raphael, and that linked French aristocratic architecture (the Louvre) with the religious architecture of the Renaissance (the Vatican). With all of those references and advocates, a welcoming entrance into heaven was surely a foregone conclusion?

Degas' laurel/basin/hat held between his legs is the earthbound sign of a more mundane heaven: having fun with your friends one summer afternoon and making art that made your friends laugh. *The Apotheosis of Degas* consciously attacks not simply one artist's silly, pompous painting, but a whole tradition of state-sanctioned, official art that had become an empty, bloated formula—empty of contemporary reality, but bloated with symbolic meaning that evoked an imaginary afterlife and reinforced the status quo in a single, apparently seamless, tableau. Ingres' painting is a vehicle for fantasy that insidiously concealed in its highly rendered realism much more than it showed. Barnes and Degas' *The Apotheosis of Degas* is a work of modern art that exposes the aesthetic, moral and political bankruptcy of that fantasy—in effect, it shatters that world and reduces it to kitsch.

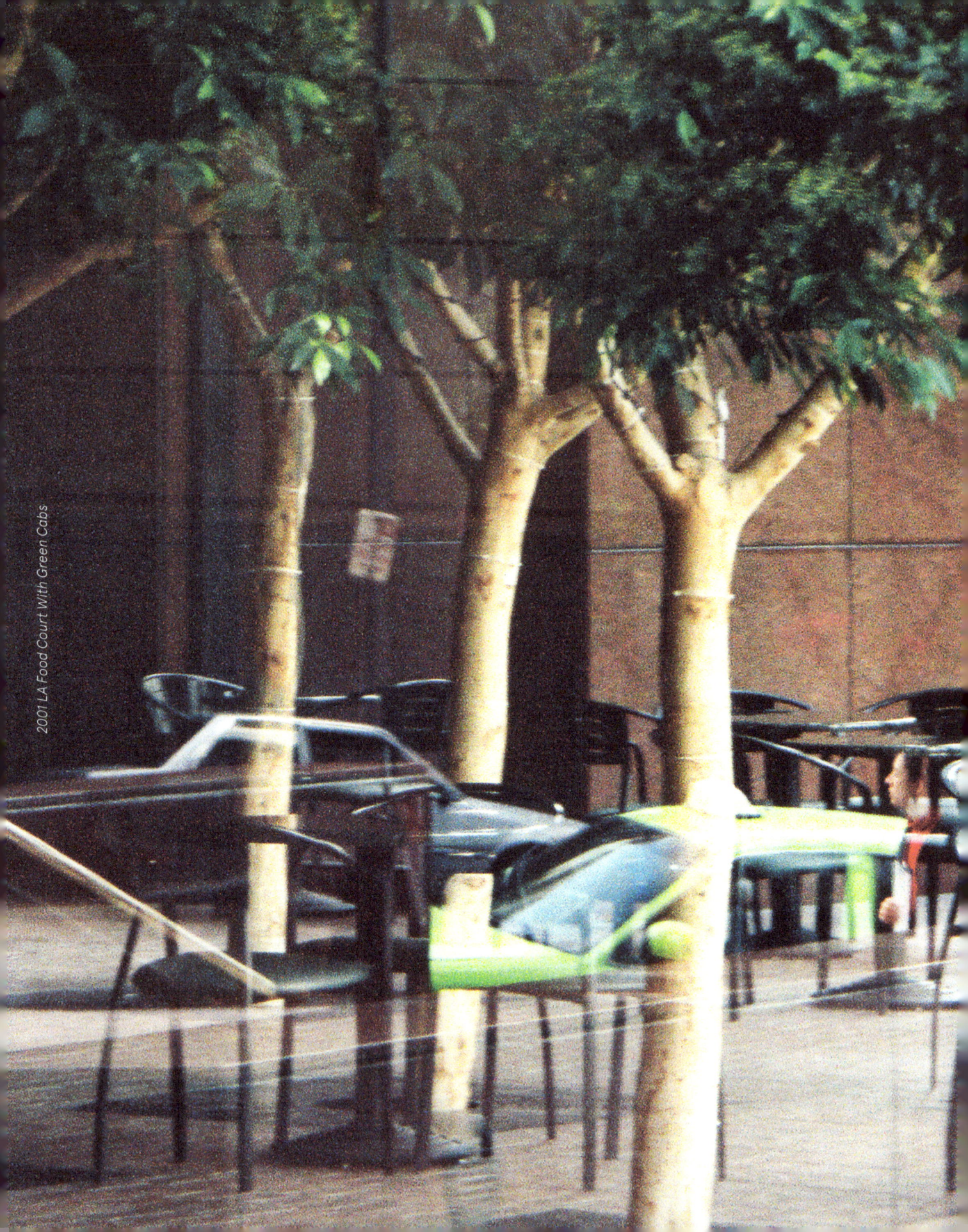

2001 LA Food Court With Green Cabs

New Palimpsests From the Zen Arcade

Colin Blodorn

There is something uncannily telling about
the wide swaths of openness that stretch
across George Porcari's series of 24 photographic collages. There is also something
natural in the tendency to notice and hang
on to these areas immediately, which impose
a sort of commanding jolt to our viewing,
temporarily bypassing our instinct to seek
the bright, colorful sections we might under
other circumstances take for granted.

They are the place made open, that gives us
an anchor to navigate the peculiar information
we ultimately move towards as we drift verti-
cally upwards and downwards across the large
sheets of printed paper.

These broad corridors are filled with a sort
of shocking ambience, a generous and curious
tactic that attests to Porcari's intimate famil-
iarity with the medium he works with and his
commitment in confounding and reinventing
the processes by which he continues to stir
in his multitude of interrelated activities.
Porcari, in a rhythm that radiates from this
central zone of departure, turns his collection

"And somewhere in all this open space there is the implicit invitation for slippages to occur and for time and space to jump erratically."

of photographs into long stretches and staccato blips which hearken to a personal history of encounters in the everyday world we are introduced to (or perhaps reintroduced to) and left to mediate through this flashing blank area.

Repeated over 24 times, we can continue on in our thoughts with confidence that this isn't merely the byproduct of a mechanical error or digital glitch, but of course the result of determined actions accumulated through decades of time and consideration. Empty areas and distorted spaces, though we might forget at times, accompany us in places and ways both subtle and deceivingly apparent, carrying a weight intrinsic to the particular qualities of its own absence.

George Steiner writes on this, defending the notion that with intention:

> *Modernist tactics make of blank spaces between the lines, whether typographically declared or inferred acoustically, as in music, something altogether different from nothingness. They can contain the suppressed, the apparently forgotten which exercises a felt pressure. They can be loaded with futurity, with potential eruption into significance on the very edge of deployment. Emptiness is made fertile, a paradox made fascinatingly actual by the speculations of string theory and dark matter cosmology on "vacuum energized."* [1]

So what exactly is happening here in this fertile emptiness of space as it collides with a photographer's street level documentation of a half-century's worth of views of Los Angeles? Perhaps it is in many ways as direct as it seems: a representation of time, pushed against properties that might through the velocity of their unseen energy pull these images into another dimension of recognition.

Los Angeles, a city filmed, photographed, and thoroughly reproduced in all sorts of streams of media, has the reputation of existing in a fictitiously ethereal and truly distorted wash of the popular consciousness. A shimmeringly dingy landscape meticulously and elaborately built through ever-growing levels of production in the studios of Hollywood and Burbank into a sprawling spectacle.

Somewhere in the same circles of geography, Porcari, meanwhile, has been capturing pictures that share a certain quality of ethereality and distortion, yet doing so by veering into a much different set of circumstances. Porcari's camera points to the most fleeting scenes of the cityscape where layers of motion are caught in moments of chance and banality; an intersection filled with traffic moving at itself, a throng of shoppers and tourists refracted through mirrors and glass, the bright sun illuminating green palm fronds in front of the bunker-like backside of a beige McDonald's, a pedestrian walking by the bus station as eyes briefly meet.

These images are indeed from the flood of visual matter we absorb absently as we are busy doing other things—probably lost in our own thoughts, perhaps flipping on the turn signal to make a turn around the corner. Benign as these bits of stimulus might seem, Porcari points to their residual effect as they are filed away in the storage rooms of our unconscious minds. Walter Benjamin quotes Marx in a prelude to section N of *The Arcade Projects*, "The reform of consciousness consists solely in...the awakening of the world from its dream about itself."

Porcari's collage prints seem to wrestle with this notion, of dream and waking, and the intertwined, self-contained collision that brings about a sense of realization. It also touches

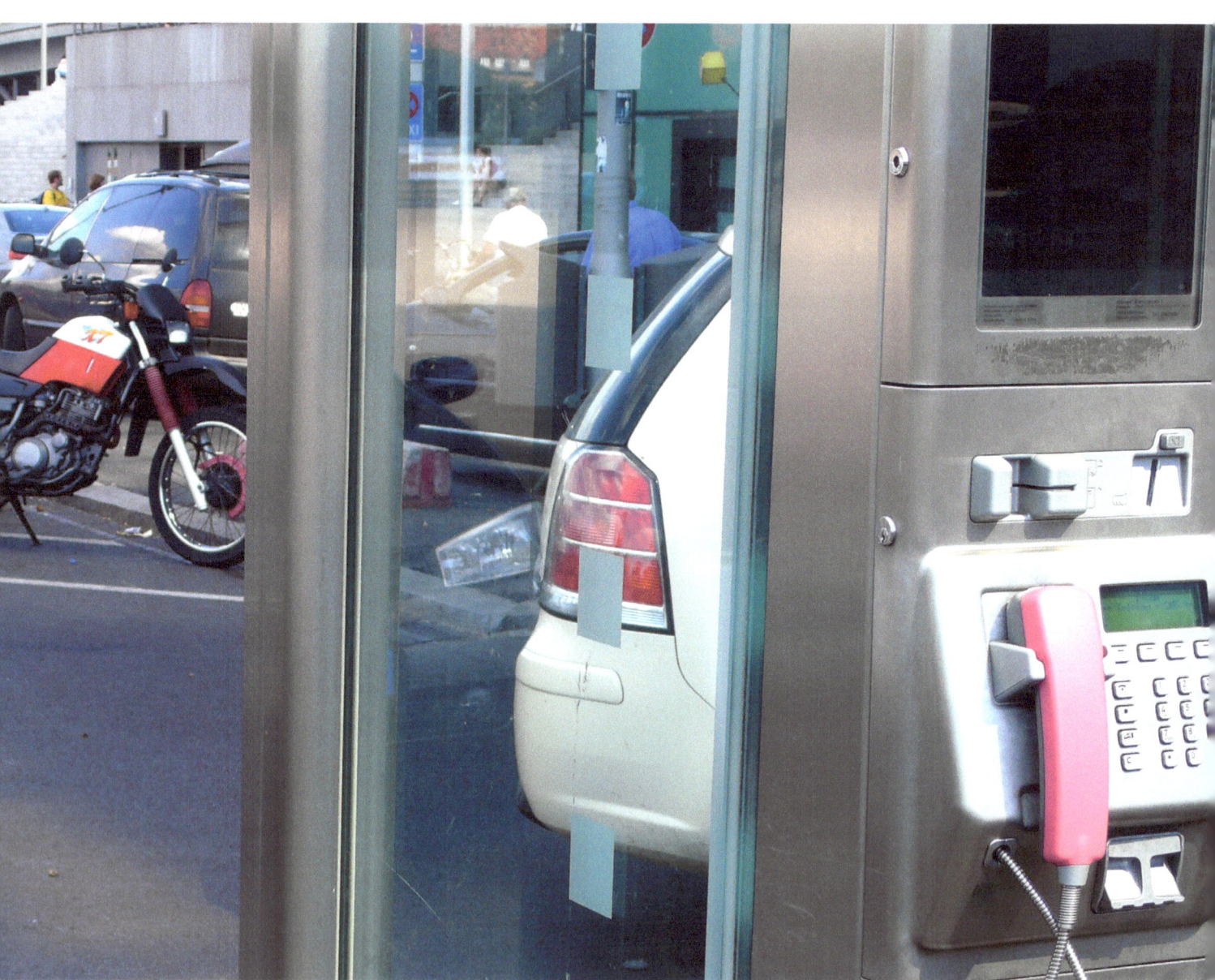

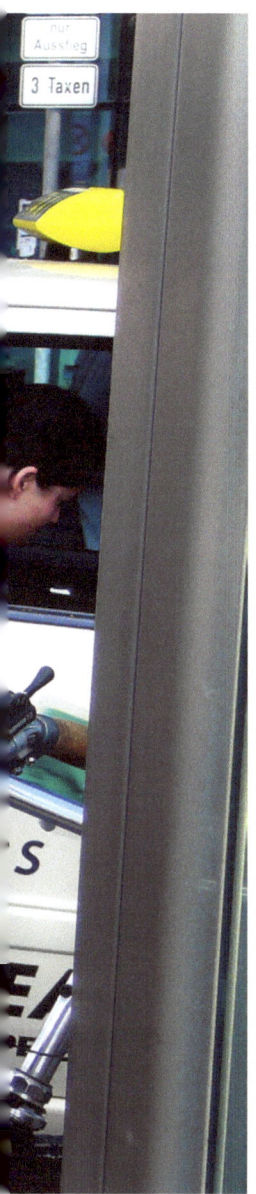

2008 Pink Public Phone

on Porcari's interest in chiseling away at the dominant structure of picture making and all it represents. Benjamin begins the section itself with a brief thought, writing "In the fields with which we are concerned, knowledge comes only in lightning flashes. The text is the long role of thunder that follows."[2]

As Porcari's blank space rhythmically shifts between opening and closing the frame, pulling us in and thrusting us out into the textual areas above and below, its conceivable we are being brought into a series of open dream-like spaces, a sort of analog to the architectural arcade made into a realm of discussion and graphic provocation. These contrasts in content and space lead to deeper fissures, which through a fragmented sequencing dialectically push these points further out into areas of more obscure possibility.

And the blank space—literally, it is paper, before anything else—white and finely textured matte paper in its pure material form, simultaneously fills the void and points to its emptiness. Left bare, highlighting its two-dimensional flatness, Porcari negates the possibility of the picture being a window to the world, as early modernists did in abstract painting and collage. The distortion

"...playing with the narrow field that separates the subject, the viewer and the author. "

of the photograph at the bottom of the page, looking like it has been siphoned through a digital cable, does something similar, pointing out its digital treatment from camera to computer screen to page, denying any illusory effect that might suggest the photographs are something other than documentations of space and time that are reproducible. (In fact many of these pictures have existed in other guises and formats over time, now scraped from those instances to appear reworked on these tableaus.)

Porcari furthers this canceling principle with digital photo printing methods by letting the ink pigments of the image sink into the paper rather than creating a gloss surface that would project both a shiny exteriority—on a more molecular level, raise the pigments above the ground of blank paper. This keeps our experience contained within the plane of the paper; it suggests in a way a reverence for the paper itself and the power it holds in its own nature. The paper is innately a site for the existence and survival of knowledge.

Knowing a bit about Porcari's personal and professional relationship to the book form and all that falls into the realm of the filmic picture form, moving or still, leads one a little ways further

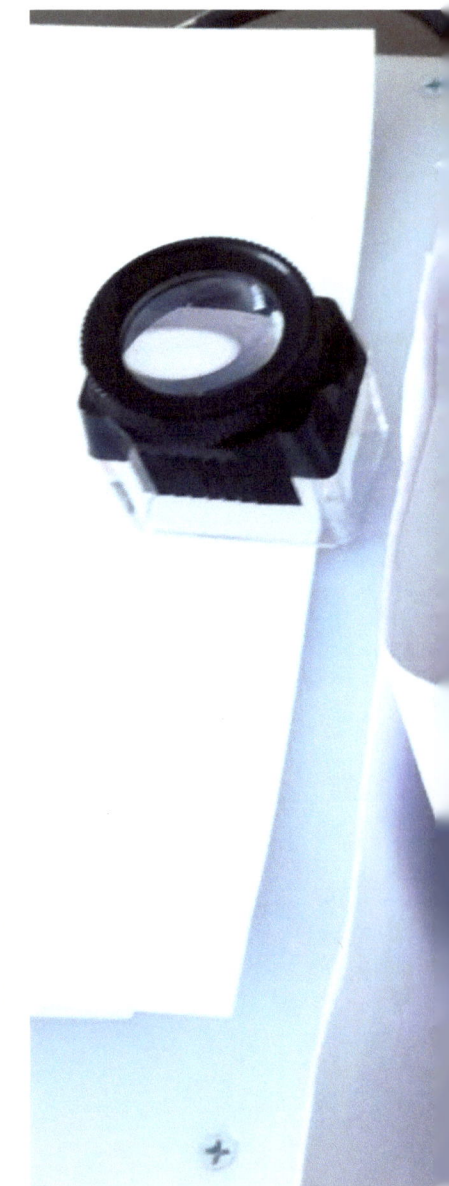

2008 Still Life With Books #21

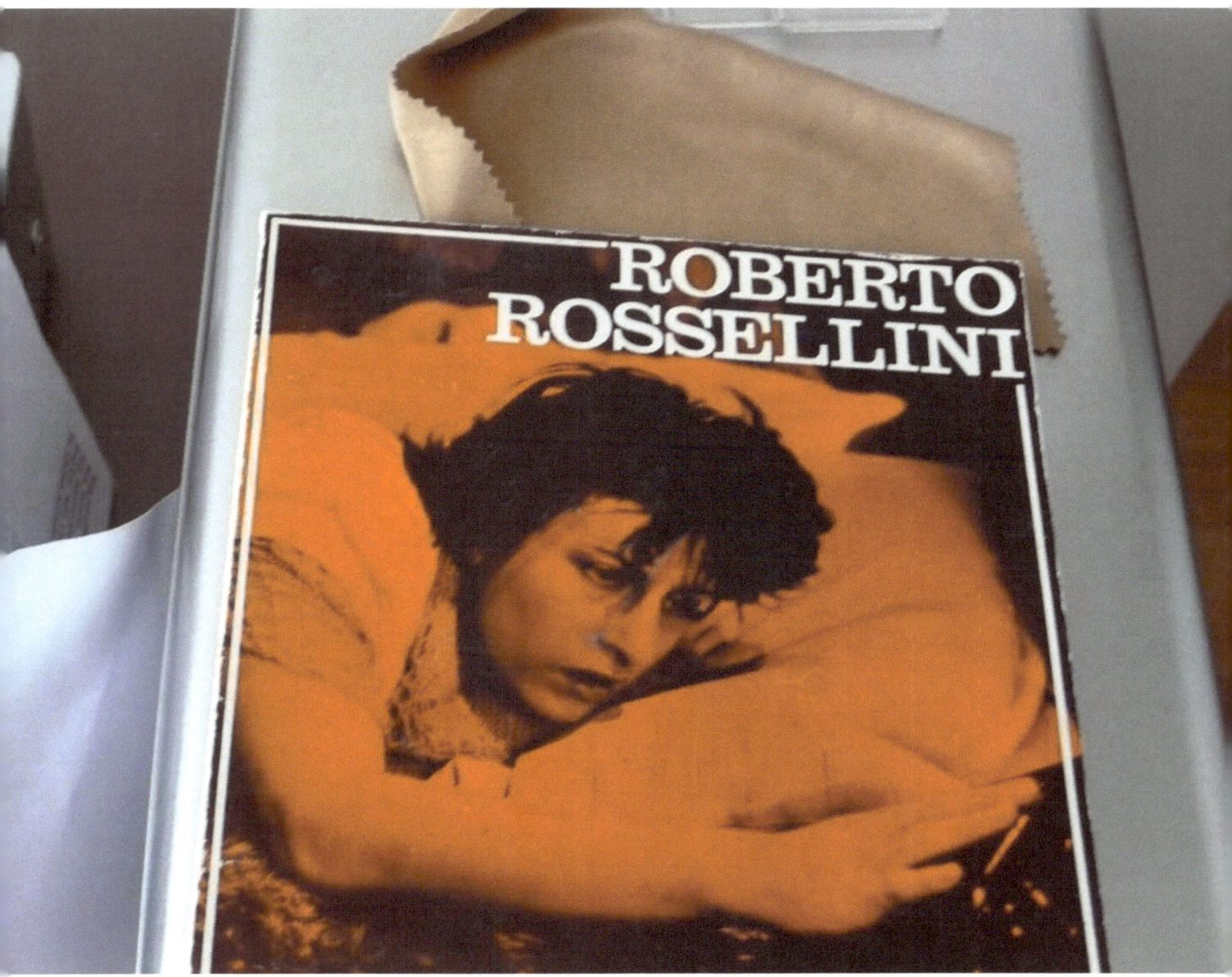

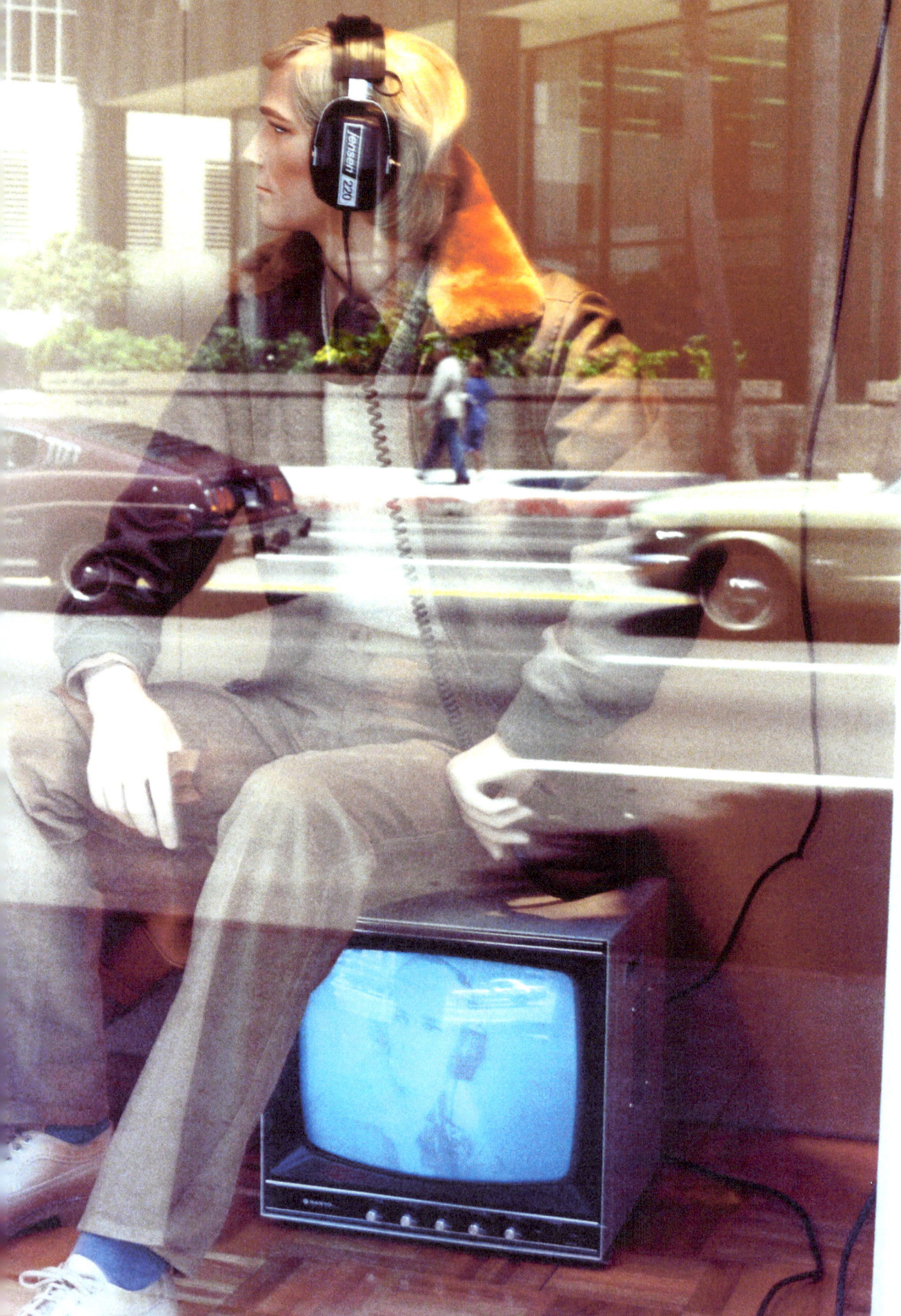

1979 LA Dummy #4

into these Saharan matte depths of paper space. One could begin to speculate towards the notion that a person is not only in some way shaped by their environment or the subject of their labors, but perhaps given enough time, begin to merge wholly with it. Porcari, who regularly rotates between the vast library of his home and the library he has gone to as a job for the last few decades, makes the case entirely plausible. He travels between landmarks composed of books, albums, films—the territory of recorded time and thought made infinite. Satchel upon the shoulder, weighted down with various books, DVDs and CDs of different periods and orders, keep Porcari tided over in the in-between zones, tools and nourishment for his greater project.

Moving between these locations, between the blank space and the photograph, between awakening and dream, the empty and loaded corridor—this modulated arcade is in a sense the site of inhabitance. It's as if the photographer points from the position of the blank space towards the area of the picture, looking out at the reflections of the world from the chambers of knowledge and information. And somewhere in all this open space there is the implicit invitation for slippages to occur and for time and space to jump erratically. In

GFLA Beverly Grove 2010, don't we see a reflection of Porcari himself, emerging from the blankness? Is it Porcari? Or perhaps an apparition of someone else from a different time—could it be Jarry? The bicycle substituted for a book bag, the pistol used to light the fellow man's pipe for a camera? (...which might come equally and as alarmingly close to one's face.)

Just as early cinema pioneers such as the Lumieres made great use of the mutability of their medium—playing it forwards and backwards, slowing it down and interrupting its linearity and logic, and playing with the narrow field that separates the subject, the viewer and the author, Porcari also levels the structures of linearity and centrality, inserting himself into the dynamic place between seeing and comprehending what we may or may not realize we're seeing.

By locating himself in the cosmos of his life-long pursuit of looking at and reading through the world around him, focusing on the areas of erasure and absence and the fringes of the periphery, he reminds us that these places, which are all too easily overlooked, contain volumes of knowledge and liberation that might be vital to awaken to.

2010 Gardena Apartments

Undesirable Alien: A Diptych

Veronica Gonzalez Peña

I

My life has, for a long time, been woven around George Porcari's, or his around mine. It is in my calling up of memory for the writing of this piece, and the corresponding implicit sadness at the passage of all that time, that I am heartened too by the ongoing quality, strength, and vitality of our interrelatedness. Yet, there is a sadness there, the past...we know that language is in some ways always an elegy for and of itself. In the moment we speak: I, I is already past.

It is mournful that gap, or due to be mourned. And if my utterance proclaims its own passing even as I begin to speak, how much more is this passing eulogized by the written word, a film, a photograph. But present too, somehow, all time collapsed, for how deeply felt, how actual as I recall it, the long ago story of our first meeting, with Steve Hanson, in the stacks of the library at Art Center College. Or the first time I met Jorge, a year or so later, at George's house, as he awkwardly walked in with a mutual friend; or, another meeting, more than a decade later, at George's house

"And so, can there be an art that is not an elegy?"

again (a different place) where Jorge first asked me out on a date; or the fact that Mark von Schlegell and I published George's first essays in what was our long ago zine, *Inflatable Magazine*. This after I had introduced Mark to many of my friends (including George) in the unlikely setting of the central market in Coyoacan, in Mexico City.

How can I look at any of George's work, or speak of the presence of the object, when what the object in and of itself most marks is a passing, a time gone, a death, a pointing away from, a not quite...not quite...Though in our less melancholic moments, these objects seem to prod toward as well; it is an incomplete set of motions, this time travel, this looking at our past, prodding toward the future, yet the gestures remain.

These questions seem central not only to our longstanding friendship but on a larger scale to George Porcari's very art. His work is so de-centered that it appears to be perpetually involved in the pointing toward that which lies beyond it; and in this directing out is implied the gap, the interstice, which we as viewers obsessively try to fill, though we know we never fully can. And so, the question remains, in his work (as in that of many others): how to con-

sider the space between, the gap, and those things, like music, or the best writing, and art, which depend on that space: on the this, to that...to that...to that. If transition, or the space between is all there is, really, then how to think about the moment, the image, the thing? Can flow and vitality have something to do with it?

There are those for whom this question of flow, of the vital, seems central, Henri Bergson helped to define this question as a question. For Bergson the interconnectedness of all things seemed the only reality; the breaking down of systems or objects into understandable and fully knowable parts (what he termed the scientific order) seemed a dark fiction indeed; for how can things be pulled out of time and thus "known"? In the moment we take things out of the vital, we are creating a fiction which we term "knowledge" or as Bergson puts it "scientific truth."

But things do not exist like that, independent of relations. How much more real the intuitive form of knowledge he espoused, with its ultimate acknowledgment of the interconnectedness of all things, of our inability to know through a breaking down into parts. Can the story of a friendship, for example, be put down to any one event, or set of events, or relation,

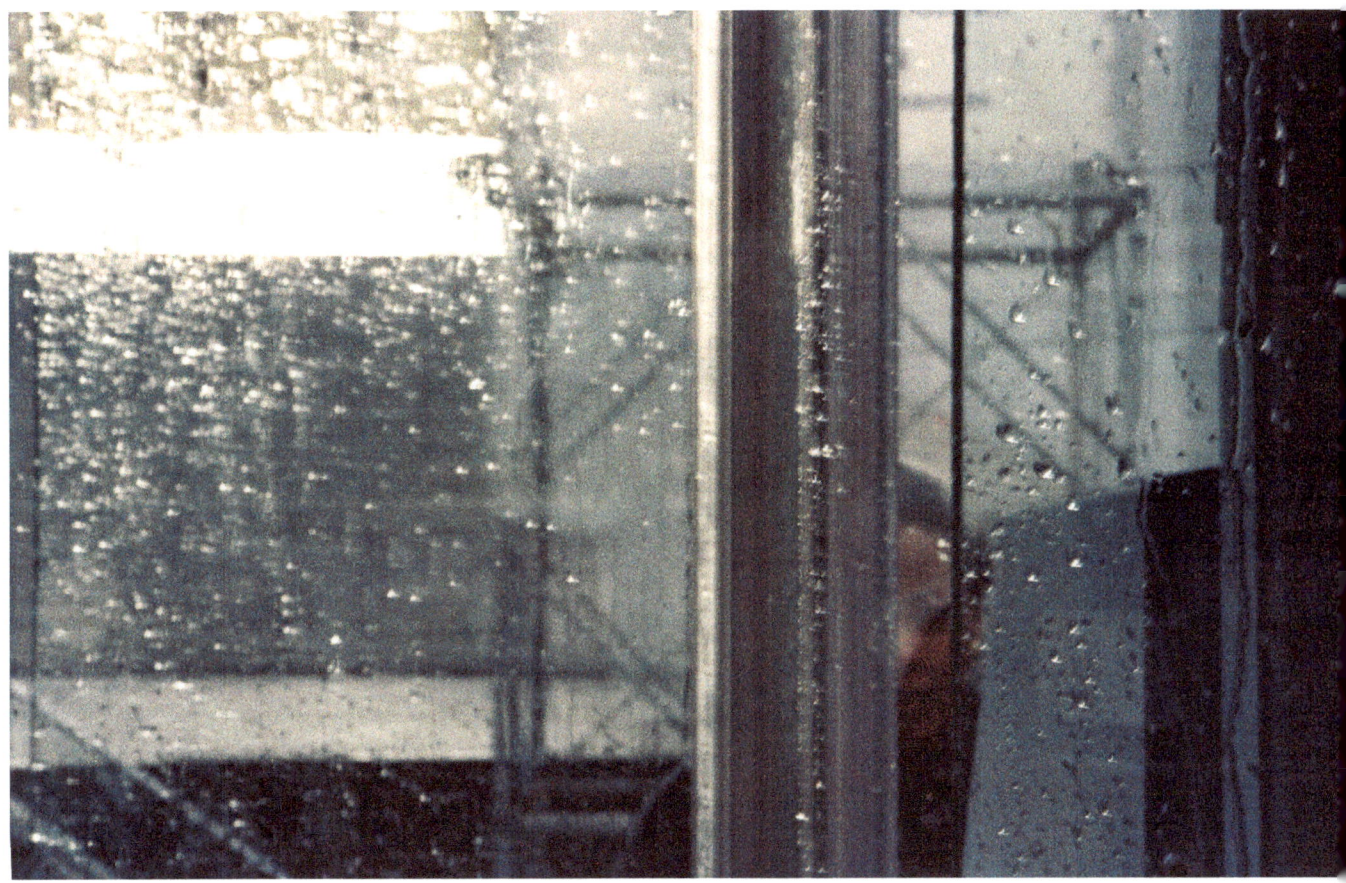

1984 Woman Waiting for a Public Phone

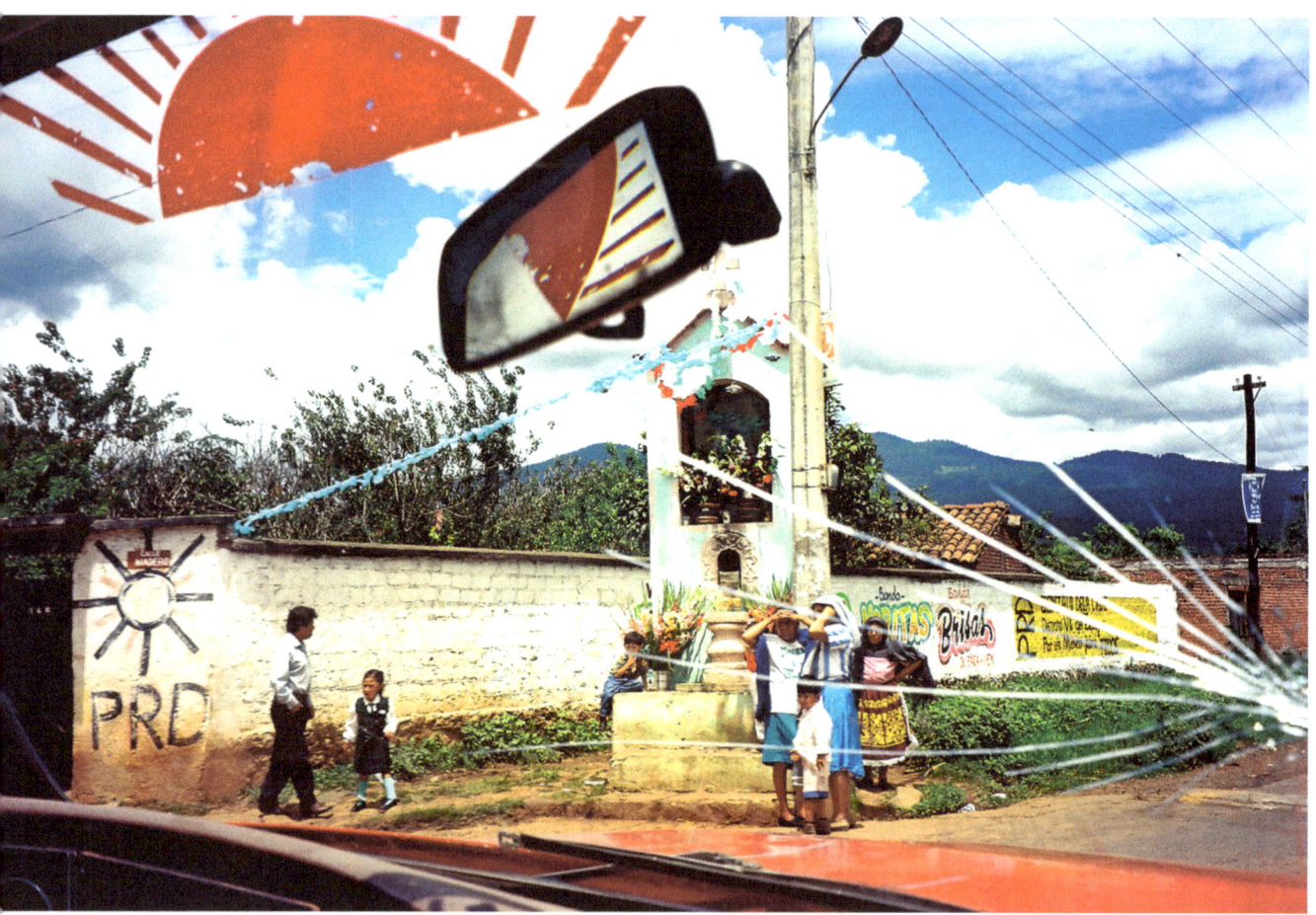

1994 Pátzcuaro

or set of relations, is it not an organic form like any other, dependent on all that touches it, and all that is brought in to it?

And so, can there be an art that is not an elegy? What if instead of notions of death, of the finished object, there is a possibility that a certain kind of art can lead us into an agreement with Bergson that knowledge is intuitive, an art which leads us to the polyphonic, to the layering of what we know, speak, see, are.

Can objects and texts in fact function in this way instead, a pointing toward, a part of the motion, a presence through interconnectedness? Film, at its core speaks to this, as does collage. A non-idealist, non-absolutist, non-gestalt, non-object obsessed, non-privileged moment, way of viewing the world which leads us instead to a view based on contingency and incompletion and process and dynamics and a moving toward.

It is Bergson who helps us to wonder: what if things cannot be broken up, not known in that way, what if it is as soon as we attempt to break things down into constituent parts, into glorified objects, that we are dealing with, causing, a real death, ignoring the this to that. Everything is connected, Bergson works to

remind us, and in an attempt to really know, you cannot pull things apart. Memory, which is invoked in all of our thoughts, helps our understanding of this, aids in our grasp of the vital motion...

George Porcari's work speaks to all of this. It is full of notions of memory—real and imagined, or fictionalized (though never contrived)—and longing, and the space between. It is de-centered, and ambiguous, and seems to strike out against the final say, the complete object. When I first met George in 1985 he was making long strips of images mounted on foam core or aluminum. He is a real film buff, and this work was certainly a nod to film; the images were a succession of family snapshots, some portraits, shots of friends, film stills, found images.

Through his placement, a succession, or motion was inscribed into these individual shots. He moved you through them, or, rather, he allowed you to move through them, at your own pace. You might recognize a teen-age George, about to board a plane leaving Lima for Los Angeles and surrounded by little girls— his cousins there to bid farewell; those girls, of various sizes, all wore the same orange dress, white piping accentuating their arms and chests, the soon to be forever altered

George standing bravely alongside them in his stoic good-bye stance. You might recognize an obscure shot from *Nosferatu*, or *Alice in the Cities*, or Glenn Gould's pointing hand. There's a smiling Steve Hanson, there's Pae White, Jorge, once or twice, there am I.

Those transitions from image to image underscore the space between, motion, vitality; the images had no easy relation so that you, as the viewer, were involved in creating the interconnectedness of it all, and you too, as the viewer, were a part of it, free to take what you would from the work. After about eight years of these long strips, sometimes with up to 50 images, George pared the work down, literally, into pairs of images.

And this in a much more controlled way, of course makes us think of collage and jazz, unlikely pairings and the this to that, and of what happens to the eye and mind when presented with two things as one. The jumps we make, like those of time (60 years between the images taken by his Tío Cesar and those taken by himself) and place (the thousands of miles between Lima and Los Angeles, or Berlin and Lima—again in the Tío Cesar series) underscore all of the visual motion in those pairings, those time traveling diptychs.

I have mentioned Tío Cesar twice now, the photographs, and so I feel I should share something about that work. Tío Cesar, George's uncle, was a medical student in Berlin, until forced to leave there as an undesirable alien in the late 1930s. He had a rough ride home, over the sea between, and died a year later from pneumonia contracted on that long boat journey back.

The photos in this series are pictures taken by him while in Berlin, the pretty girlfriend, a love left behind (much as George would many years later leave his pretty cousins) whom none of the family ever met. Did she ever find out Cesar had died? No one knows her, so how could they have contacted her?—these photographs are all we have of that love.

George recently told me that he believes the deep melancholia which permeated his family as he was growing up was due to Cesar's untimely death, the golden son, to be sure, and his family's inability to get over that loss. Sixty years later George would have a dialogue with this long lost uncle, who had sepia-colored so much of his life but whom he had never met; in those diptychs George answers his uncle's photographs with images he has himself taken, mostly of Los Angeles—

feeling half alien himself here, the immigrant with one foot in each of the Americas for his entire life. George has a great love for *La Jetée*. I understand this love more deeply now: the undesirable, the woman left behind, the attempt to try to reach her, the photographs— for one moment instilled with life—the here but not here aspect of it all, a moving toward which can never be fulfilled.

It was after these diptychs that George moved to the single image, yet he is still able to create a motion in these single image shots, a de-centered feeling which defies the heroic he is so ardently against. He does this through his repeated use of reflection, through his images which are so often cut up by a telephone pole, or a doorway, a bus stand, or a moving vehicle; the way that he manages to create a collage effect through the use of buses, road signs, moving cars and mirrors, is quite remarkable.

But there is the melancholic air of all of the subjects as well—for melancholy always points out, to something missing, so that we seldom get a subject completely caught up in an action, completely and fully in and of themselves—instead, in the few instances where there is a subject at all, there seems also to be a gap, an unapproachable space.

The photographs do seem to mark a death, to be a sort of elegy, a mournful death poem, his uncle forever eulogized, even when there is nothing of him within the frame of the shot.

So, Steve Hanson introduced us. He and George both worked in the library at Art Center (which has become such a mythic place, so many people following in their footsteps— Diana Thater, and Giovanni Intra and Jorge, and Mark von Schlegell—whom I prodded to ask Steve for a job). Steve and I were reading incessantly in those days; there was a great used bookstore we would all go to together, and about which George has since made a film, *House of Fiction*. We were just taking everything in; and George was helping to contextualize; he was our informal teacher, our mad professor friend.

In those days we listened to a lot of music too; Steve and I had been LA punks; we'd met several years before at a Black Flag show when I was still in high school—well, the band never showed up (they were supposed to play at his school, La Cañada High), but we were both there. By 1987 we were living together, with a painter who was a protégé of Jeremy Gilbert Rolfe's, and we had a lot of parties. Steve's great art band, Myther, played their first show

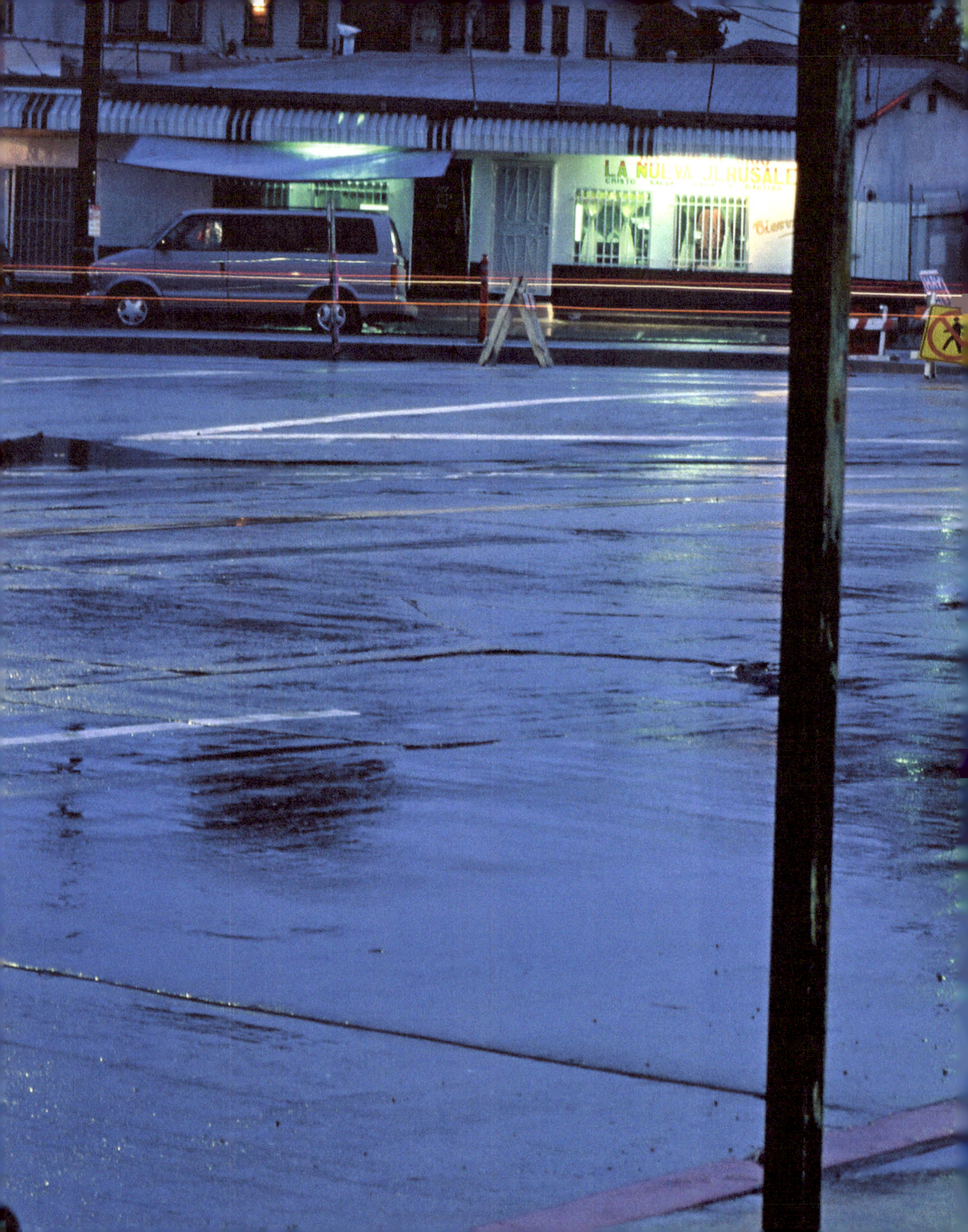

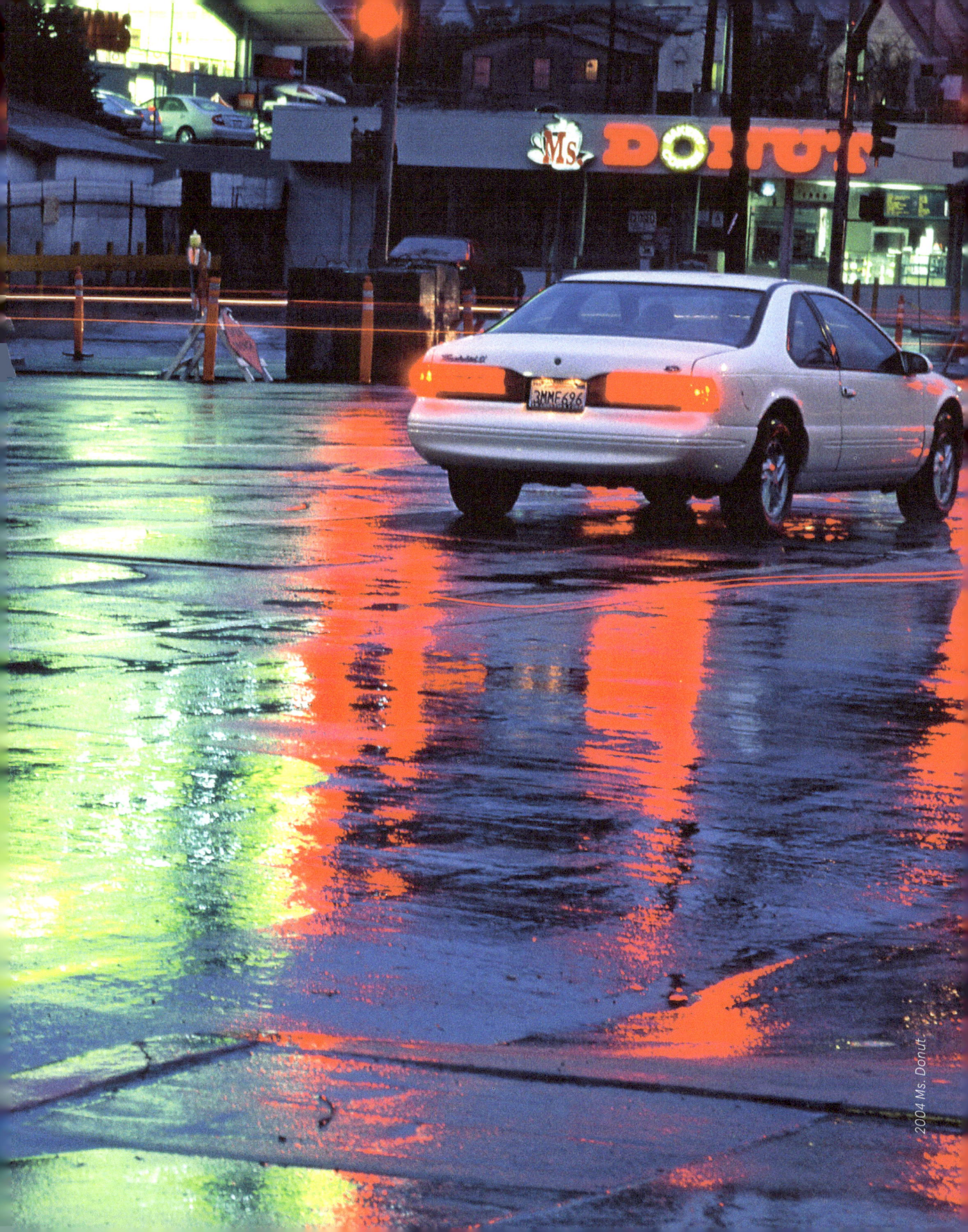

2004 Ms. Donut

"In becoming a participant in these transitional open spaces an activation, which is life, occurs."

in our living room. George was there for all of this, again, contextualizing, talking about NY in the 70s, comparing us to his friends back then. He is a great lover of jazz, and though at that point I knew nothing about that music, I would later come to understand where it meets with his love of collage, and sampling and incomplete thoughts—because incompletion seems to be the only place to leave a thought. As mentioned I met Jorge with George. I remember we were all sitting on the floor of George's apartment and Jorge came in with my and Steve's painter roommate.

A month or so later I saw Jorge's first show at Bliss, in the garage, which Steve and Jorge and George all helped to drywall. It was a great show—I've written about it elsewhere—and when I complimented Jorge on it he awkwardly kicked some pebbles around and shyly thanked me without looking up.

Nearly 15 years later it would be as we were leaving George's house that Jorge would ask me out on our first date. I thought he was joking, we'd known each other so long at that point. Of course, it turns out he wasn't; Penelope, our daughter, is the proof of that. George Porcari showed work at Bliss too, the aluminum mounted fifty image homage to

Death in Venice, simply titled Death in Venice, a piece in four or five long strips—the Luchino Visconti film with Dirk Bogarde is based on Gustav Mahler; Porcari humorously bases his Death in Venice on Stravinsky and his wife vacationing in Venice, a much lighter version of love, which George ends with a snapshot photograph he took on a beach of a dog.

This exemplifies his disdain for the heroic; he is a funny flaneur, has an admiration of the space between things, of process, openness; he has a deep love of collage, is a teacher, a talker, and a great listener too. There is, to be sure, a lot of silence with him. A lot of observing. But when you hear a voice slightly different from the others, and interrupt to ask a question: Tell me about this woman singing? he will go on to tell you the entire history of Sathima Bea Benjamin, of her husband, Dollar Brand, and her one existing recording, made with Brand and Duke Ellington.

Or if you make a comment: I just saw Nights of Cabiria for the first time, he will tell you how the film came about, Giulietta Masina mugging for the camera during the shooting of La Strada and how Fellini decided to make a film based on those expressive faces, Masina's funny Charlie Chaplin games. Or he will begin to speak about a beautiful poet you are both staring at in a book; and there is a love of life in this. A generosity. A spirit that revels in the world it inhabits and wants to give some of that back to you, like any one of your favorite friends who pulls out all their books and hands you a mix-tape as a gift the moment you walk into their room. You enter a space in this way; share an interior, and this in-between space, the space which is his because he is offering it to you and yours because you are receiving and participating in it too, and neither of yours because it is shared and you are both open and offering and giving and talking.

This shared space is the locus of creativity, the great child psychologist, D.W. Winnicott, tells us, the space in which life is lived in an active mode. The gap, the transition, the space of non-ownership, the space of motion. The transitional space, Winnicott calls it. And in becoming a participant in these transitional open spaces an activation, which is life, occurs.

There is a sense of freedom, of life, of choice, inscribed into Bergson's insistence that we consider the temporal, duration. And it is in this spirit that George Porcari's work provides us with a dynamic layering of information, each image pointing us in a multitude of directions, activating the space with our own memories, chance encounters (it is helpful in this vein to know that Porcari doesn't stage his images), literary and filmic and musical references, a cacophony of images in each single shot. This vitality is often and poetically hinted at through his use of reflections, a trope he has been employing since the 1970's.

II

Then Joana understood that the utmost beauty was to be found in succession, that movement explained form—it was so high and pure to cry: movement explains form!—and pain was also to be found in succession because the body was slower than the movement of uninterrupted continuity.

—Clarice Lispector, *Near to the Wild Heart*

George's newest work, *Greetings From LA*, plays with these notions of time travel and the space between in ways even more extreme. They are single image "collages," once again, so much happening in the space of one image that it is hard to make out what is actually going on;

surely the pictures are manipulated? Though after spending some time with an image like *Arts District 2011*, we finally begin to understand that what we are looking at is a series of deferrals, a series of reflections: through windows, and mirrors and parked cars. The bald man is sitting in a restaurant, we begin to understand, his interlocutor not visible, a police man with a billy club outside that window, tiny and reflected in a car's side-view mirror is revealed another cop, his body and badge floating at a strange angle; and then we realize that all of it is somehow simultaneously grounded and being thrown off balance by a single white bike. A de-centering and confusing multitudinous image of contemporary urban life.

After a pause, we see there is a strange elongated image, looking almost like a gestural set of colors, sitting beneath a great expanse of white space. What is that white space? And we come to see that this strange flattened image is in fact an elongated version of the one we have just been figuring out, the one that sits above all that white, "it is as if we are traveling faster than time, almost, so that what we are looking at is what we would see if we could time travel, the things we leave behind stretched by the astronomical speed at which we are traveling..." and as he says this to me I realize that George Porcari is still dealing with loss, with the gap between, simultaneously, within the space of one piece, of one image, making the moment we see clearly up above, turn into the moment of swift motion, of what we are already leaving behind, squashed and stretched as if by the rapidity of our departure, past and present there at the same time, with that great white space of mourning, of loss, sitting there between.

It is, in his images, as if all time exists and has already passed at once...or is in the state of passing; and we are always in the desperate act of holding on. Loss is inscribed into everything we see, that white space tells us, and this space of nothing, of mourning and of longing and melancholic desire is what is most present as we try to grasp at the image that slips away beneath us...even as we try to decipher and grab it...

We can't help but imagine George as the little boy in *Gardena 1976*, eyeing us curiously from the back of a brown station wagon as he is being driven off, in the wrong direction... Gardena is where George landed as a boy, we know, a cautiously curious, surely confused, transplant from Peru. And then there he is

"It is, in his images, as if all time exists and has already passed at once...or is in the state of passing; and we are always in the desperate act of holding on. Loss is inscribed into everything we see, that white space tells us, and this space of nothing, of mourning and of longing and melancholic desire is what is most present as we try to grasp at the image that slips away beneath us...even as we try to decipher and grab it..."

again, underneath himself, below all that white space of loss, of what he's left behind, those pretty cousins; there he is, stretched and elongated by the speed of time, squashed by what he has left and is continually leaving...and we come to understand that in the moment we look at him, in the moment we think of him, he is always and still both fully there, that transplanted, time traveling boy, fully there, and already gone.

What is to make a mark, distort it, and then erase it, all at the same time? In these pieces the erasure, the white space of disappearance is so much bigger than the images which border it. George does give the urban image back to us, deformed; speed and motion disfigure he tells us. And for an immigrant this is an interesting sensibility. Motion distorts. Who knows this better than an immigrant? In your departure everything will change; your world will never be the same; you will always be between that which you have left and what you are going toward...the white space, the space between, will be large and unspeakable, it will threaten to overtake the moment, pointing always toward the tragedy of constantly leaving behind, which is time...

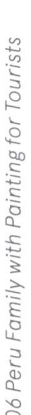

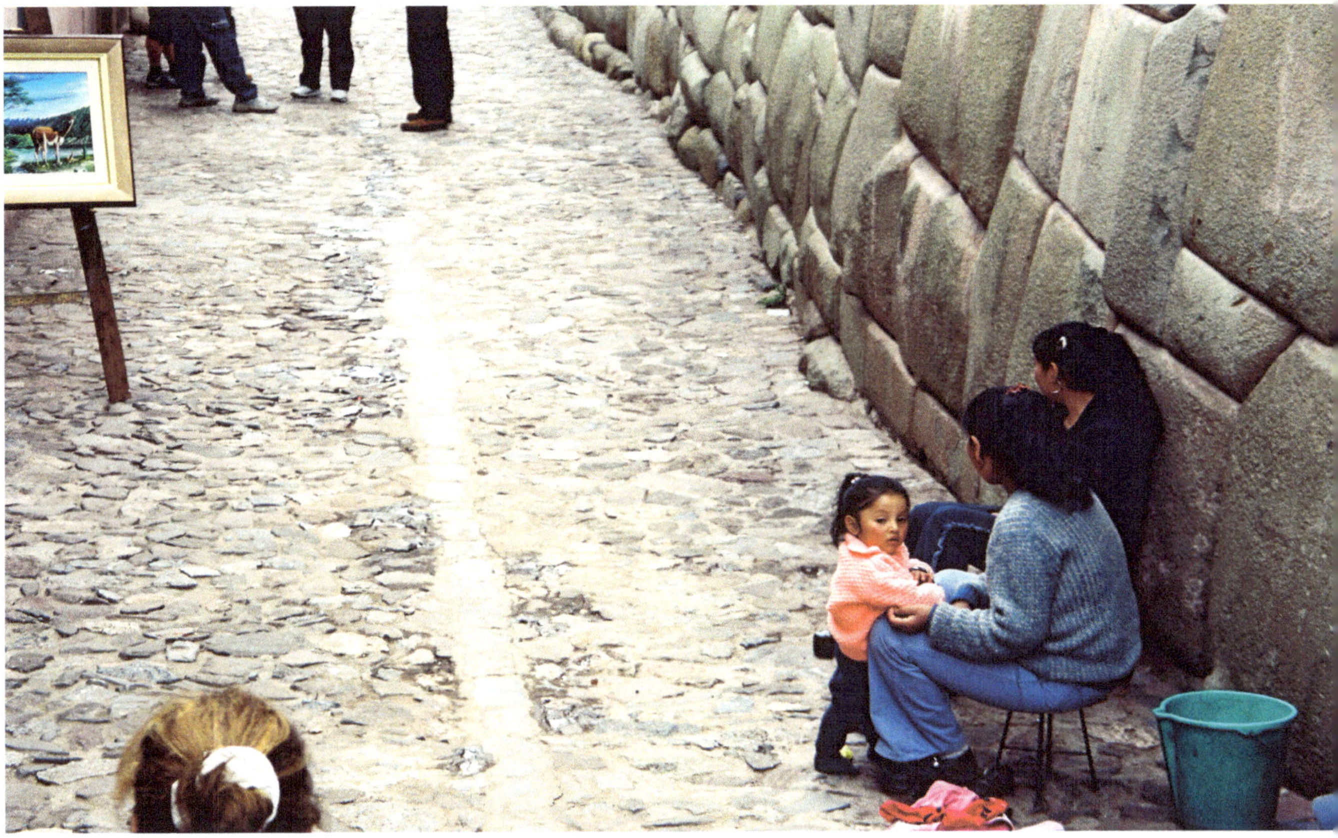

2006 Peru Family with Painting for Tourists

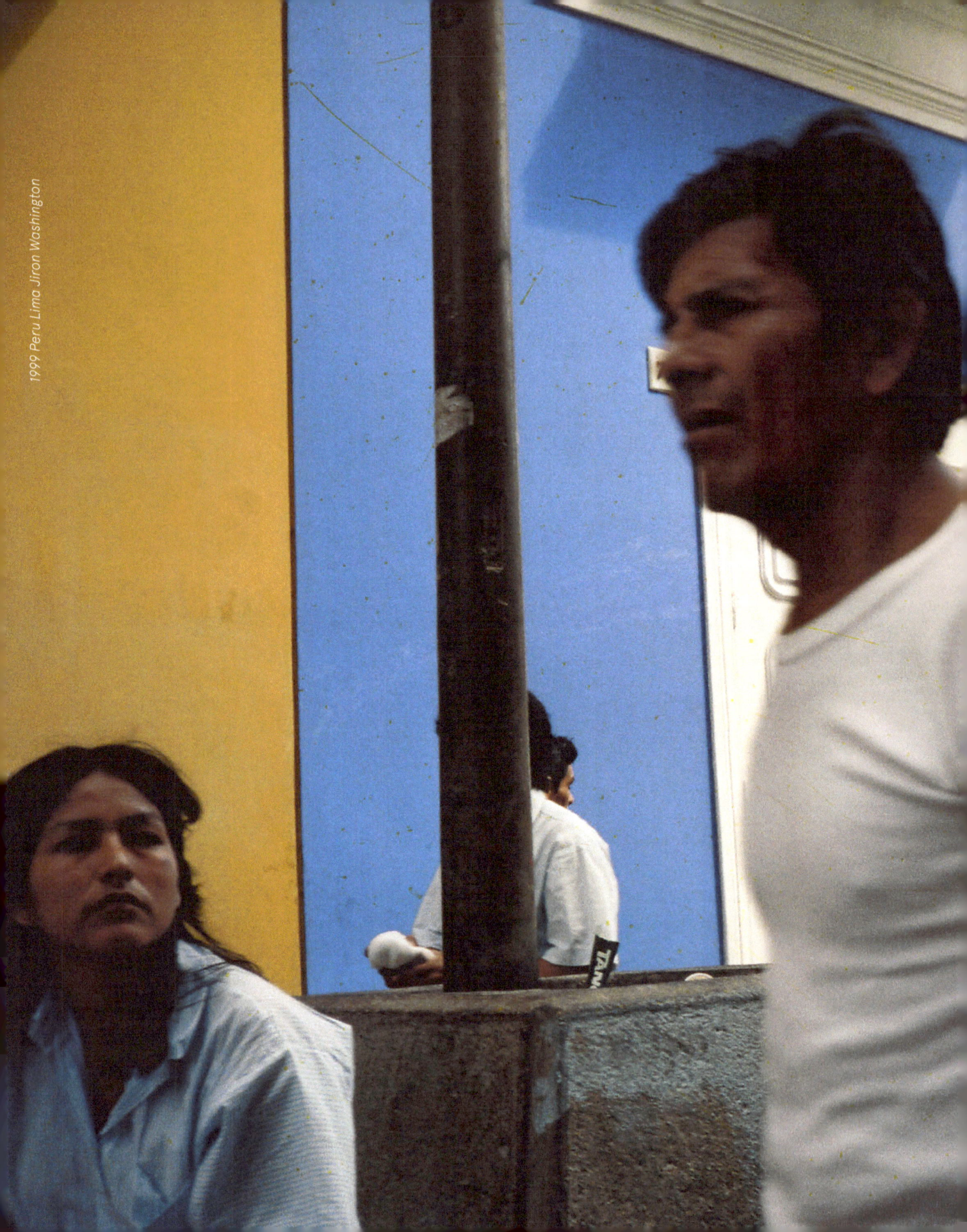

1999 Peru Lima Jiron Washington

The Delight of the Particular:
The Photography of Ronald Traeger

George Porcari

The pictures were, for the most part, meant to be seen in fashion magazines and the connotation is that this is a programmatic, institutional activity—the code of fashion images is inscribed in us. As we know its major functions are to give pleasure, to amuse, to educate, to create material needs, to reassure and to help us conform. Yet within this rigid commercial matrix, there is room for ideas to come into play, which is why a fashion picture by David LaChapelle looks very different from one by Wolfgang Tillmans. As Roland Barthes said in *The Photographic Message* "...every code is both arbitrary and rational; all recourse to a code is therefore a way for humanity to prove itself, to test itself through a rationality and a liberty."[1] It is in that space of play before the image congeals into codes that photographers are relatively free. This essay explores the work of one such photographer who worked briefly from 1962 to 1967.

Ronald Traeger's pictures are dramatic and quotidian, ambiguous and matter-of-fact, playful and philosophical. The pictures seem to participate in a holistic sense with the people and the spaces that he photographs, and this world-view is not so much illustrated as made concrete in the work itself. They express a philosophy of life and tell us about the world Traeger saw: a fragmentary space in continuous flux that we can perceive only by being a part of that flux; perception requires us to be a participant.

This phenomenology is made tangible in the present tense as a form of play. Of course these kinds of juxtapositions of differences that Traeger employed were seen before in pictures, such as those by Louis Faurer, Diane Arbus, Saul Leiter or Robert Frank. But in their work, these urban fragments were often perceived to express estrangement and displacement.

Even contemporary photographers, such as Anne Eickenberg or Nick Waplington, work along similar lines as those set by the New York School—that is, they are primarily about chance encounters, alienation and the absurd. With Traeger, on the contrary, these paradoxes are perceived pleasurably—even ecstatically—not

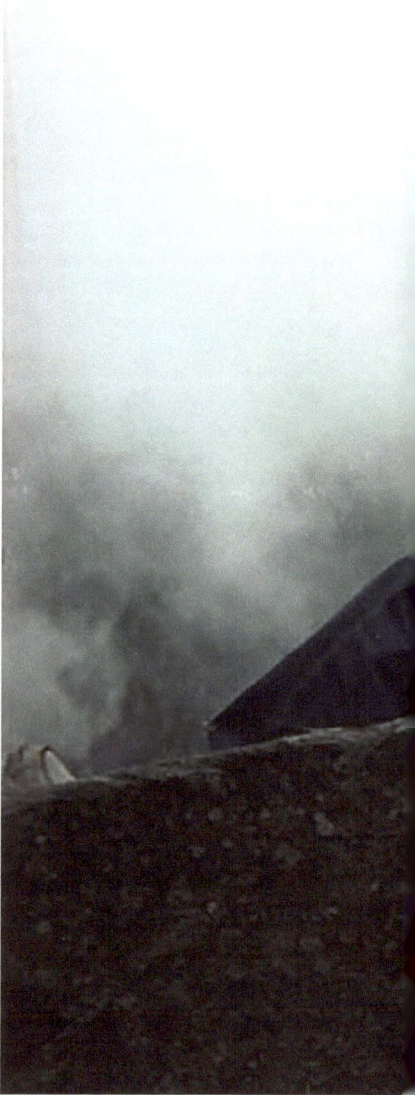

1999 Peru Young Tourist

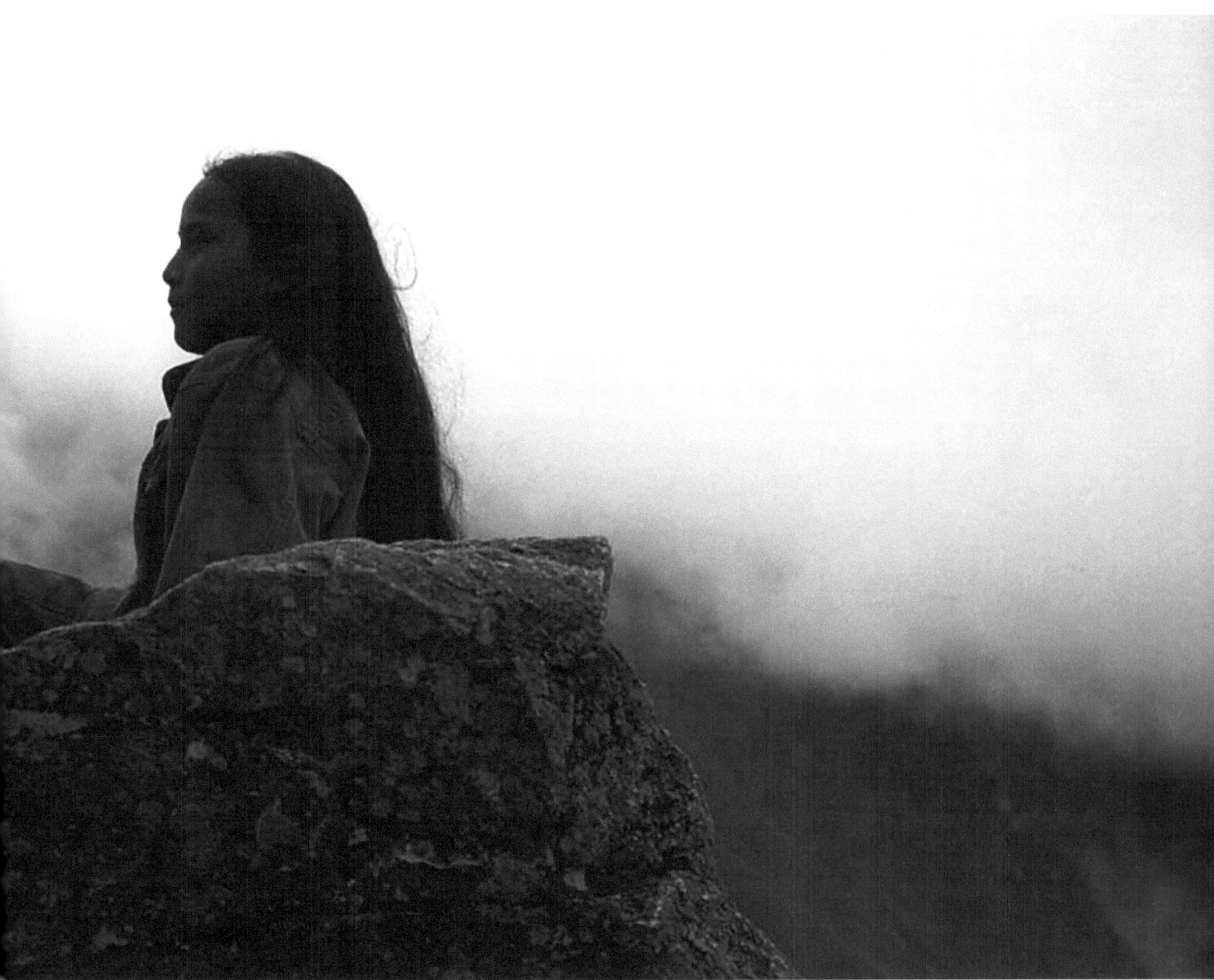

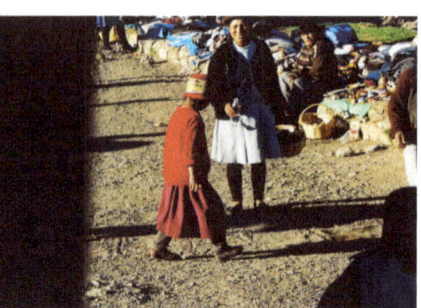

1999 Peru People Seen From a Tourist Bus

as a withdrawal from the world, but as a way back into it. The humanism is genuine because it is articulated in the way the pictures are composed, rather than imposed or illustrated. How did Traeger accomplish this balancing act between play and philosophy, between the decisive moment and theany-instant-whatever?

The work of many young photographers in the world of fashion, fine art and advertising now look like the kind of self-conscious, ironic, artificial tableaus that Traeger and his colleagues so carefully avoided, even at a cost to their commercial careers. It is those slick, turgid, post-war tableaus of Norman Parkinson, Clifford Coffin and Cecil Beaton, among many others, that the younger photographers sought to overcome, and perhaps to overthrow. There was a need to transcend that icy, affected artificiality and get at something tangible and real—something alive, factual, spiritual and bluntly corporeal—it was in the air. The Beat Generation writers felt it, as did the younger composers of pop music who wanted to eradicate the artifice of sentimental conventions and get at that essential thing; but what was that thing, and how did one get to it using photography or words or music? These were the primary questions of the young artists coming into their own during that crucial transition period, from the late 1950s to the early 1960s, as they looked around at the world they were in: post-war, post-Hiroshima, post-Gutenberg, post-Abstract Expressionism, post-Steichen's "Family-of-Man," and in the midst of an electronic revolution of which television was merely the tip of the iceberg. How did Traeger's pictures come about, what was he trying to do with them, what was the social context in which they were created, and what makes them so contemporary?

Before London there was France and Rome and before that Los Angeles. Trained at ArtCenter College in Pasadena, California, Traeger, along with four friends, founded the Globecombers, a group whose reason for being was—explicit in the name—to get out of LA as soon as possible. The school lacked inspiration, and like most art schools then and now, was reliant on rules, traditions and an unspoken submission to certain conventions.

ArtCenter, in particular, was known for a highly standardized commercial track that sought to place photographers within a viable existing market. While that is certainly a worthy aspiration, more adventurous souls might feel trapped—hence the Globecombers. After a year, Traeger and his friends set sail for Europe,

where his life would be transformed. After a few months in Rome and Paris, where he worked briefly for *Elle* magazine, he eventually settled in London, where he met his future wife Tessa Grimshaw. Unlike his contemporaries, who had very long careers, Traeger died tragically of Hodgkins disease in 1968 at the age of 32. His wife, who wrote a biography of this period and their time together in Europe, survives him, and she, along with Martin Harrison, published a book about his work in 1999.

Martin Harrison: "Although assignments occasionally came their way...they (the Globecombers) mostly photographed speculatively in the hope of their work being syndicated...the photographs that Traeger made in 1962 of the changing influence of Church and State in Rome evolved into an important body of work, his first mature achievement. The series was completed in four months of intense activity..."[2]

Traeger was twenty-five. A short time later he would move to Paris and try and make a go of it, getting some assignments for portrait and fashion work at *Elle*. Eventually he would settle in London where he worked regularly for *Vogue* alongside the photographers of his own

"Nobody can commit photography alone."

—Marshall McLuhan

generation. David Bailey, Terence Donovan and Brian Duffy formed the "terrible trinity," a term coined by the press of the time.[3] The young photographers were also called "East Enders," which was a phrase that not only described a district in London but signified the working class; an important distinction in still parochial Great Britain. While previous generations of British photographers, most famously Cecil Beaton, had come from the upper classes, and were featured regularly in traditional journals such as *Picture Post* and *Life*, the "terrible trinity" wore their working class origins on their sleeve. A brief window of opportunity had opened in the rigid class system in England that was also happening in art, film, literature, theater and music.

These photographers were part of a larger cultural revolution that included the Angry Young Men that rejected the staid mannerisms of the English theater and brought in a stark realism in their plays that actually assimilated how people actually spoke and how they were silent. The Kitchen Sink and the Free Cinema movement in England were part of a wide ranging series of "new-waves" from France to Brazil that completely revolutionized how films were made and directly challenged the status quo of Hollywood and what Francoise Truffaut

ironically called "the cinema of quality." There was a whole new approach from the post-war era, as the new pop art paintings dealt with everyday life and popular culture in a much more sarcastic and direct approach, acknowledging the broad range of image repertoire in the world at large—we see this in works by Richard Hamilton, Derek Boshier, Pauline Boty and Eduardo Paolozzi, who were making pop art collages as early as the late 1940s, and who founded The Independent Group in 1952. Most famously there was the studio work of pop groups that would revolutionize and reinvent contemporary music, leaving the formulaic rock created by impresarios far behind, as well as the staid formalism of contemporary classical music which retreated to academia, where it resides today (with a shroud of text in place of a tomb). What was happening in the arts and pop music was in fact taking place in all areas of the arts and humanities, bringing down social barriers that the ruling classes considered sacred markers.

As to be expected, there would be a push back against these new, often radical ideas, that would develop over the following decades. In the sixties, these young photographers took on portraiture, journalism and fashion, and because of their youth and quick rise to prominence, came to be known as "The Young Meteors."[4] This group consisted of people as different as Don McCullin and David Bailey, Nigel Henderson and Penny Tweedie, one of the few women photographers then working and showing regularly. Despite their differences, they all shared a similar aesthetic concern with everyday life that was depicted in a way that seemed unaffected by formal or flâneur strategies. While these qualities were not completely absent, they remained in the background, leaving center stage to a content that was often harshly realistic, with all of the inconsistencies and rough edges left in place, and without a clear, narrative arc that explained the action. What was highly unusual, and now unthinkable, was that this body of work was disseminated to the public at large via the popular magazines of the period, including the influential *Sunday Times Magazine*, on a regular weekly basis.

The approach that the young British photo-journalists in the 1960s took was blunt and confrontational, with both their subjects and their viewers. They were fearless and relentless and the resulting images were often brilliant, direct and profoundly disturbing. A good example is Don McCullin's ferocious portrait: *Homeless, Aldgate, East End, London* (1963). This extraordinary image on first glance might appear to be a snapshot, due to the homeless man's seemingly casual entrance into the frame at an angle, but a closer look proves otherwise. The man, covered in filth and with a bandaged right hand, looks thoughtfully at McCullin's camera, which frames his head. He is literally caught between church and factory; between the man and this civilized modernist oasis, is a wasteland of mud and debris.

Another example is Ian Berry's *A Mission's Failure* (1963) for the *London Times*. Berry depicts a young missionary sent to a care facility in South London, and his disastrous confrontation with men who were angry, fatigued and who saw the priest as an authority figure that they could finally lash out at. Berry's intense image captures the violence of the scene through both the older man's helpless frustration and the young priest's shock and uncertainty as to how to proceed.

The Young Meteors were able to express the moral ambiguities, mysterious narratives that lead nowhere and dramatic/comical collisions of cultures and classes into a poetics of urban space without resorting either to cloying narrative clues or to painterly references common to Pictorialism. Their often highly

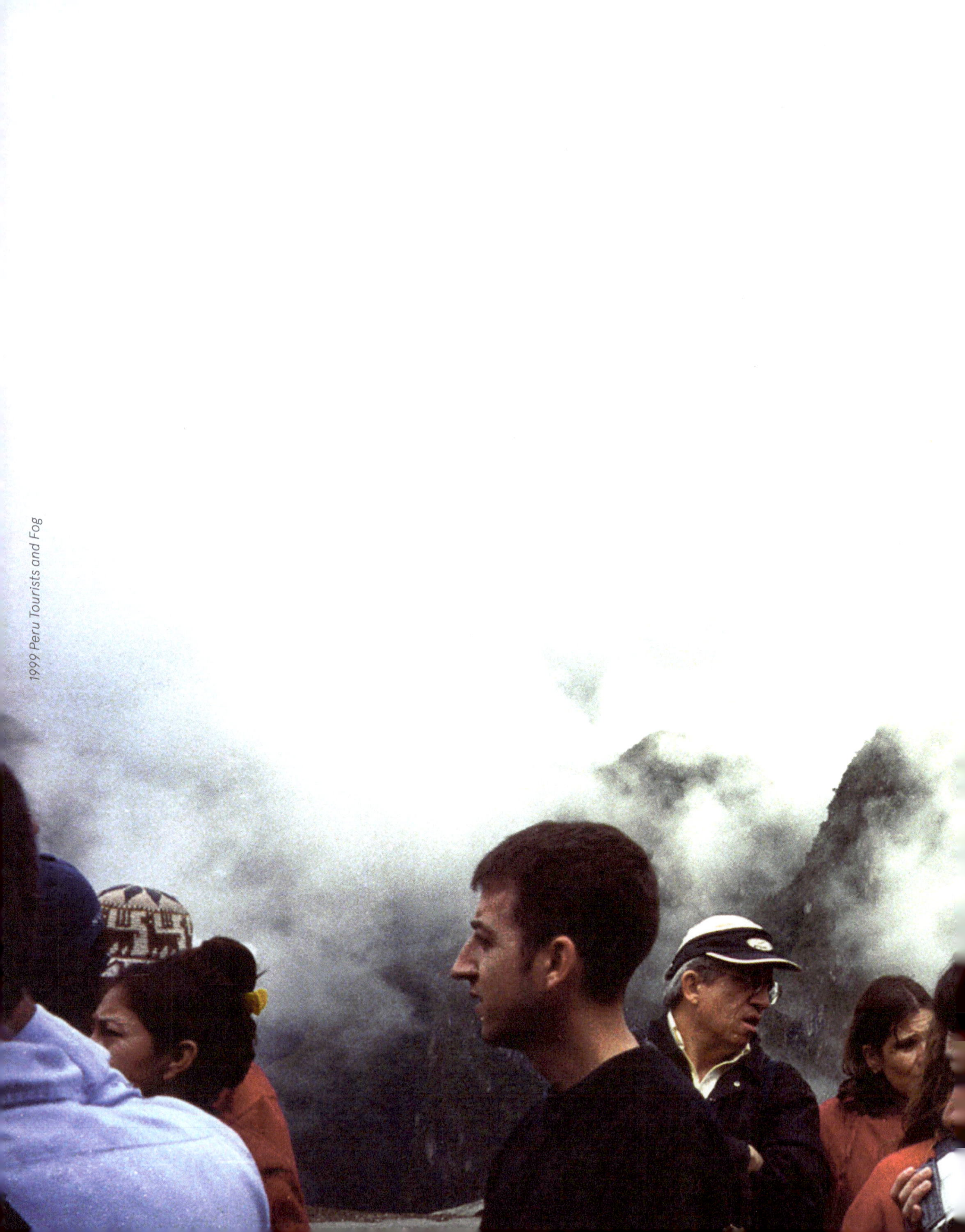

1999 Peru Tourists and Fog

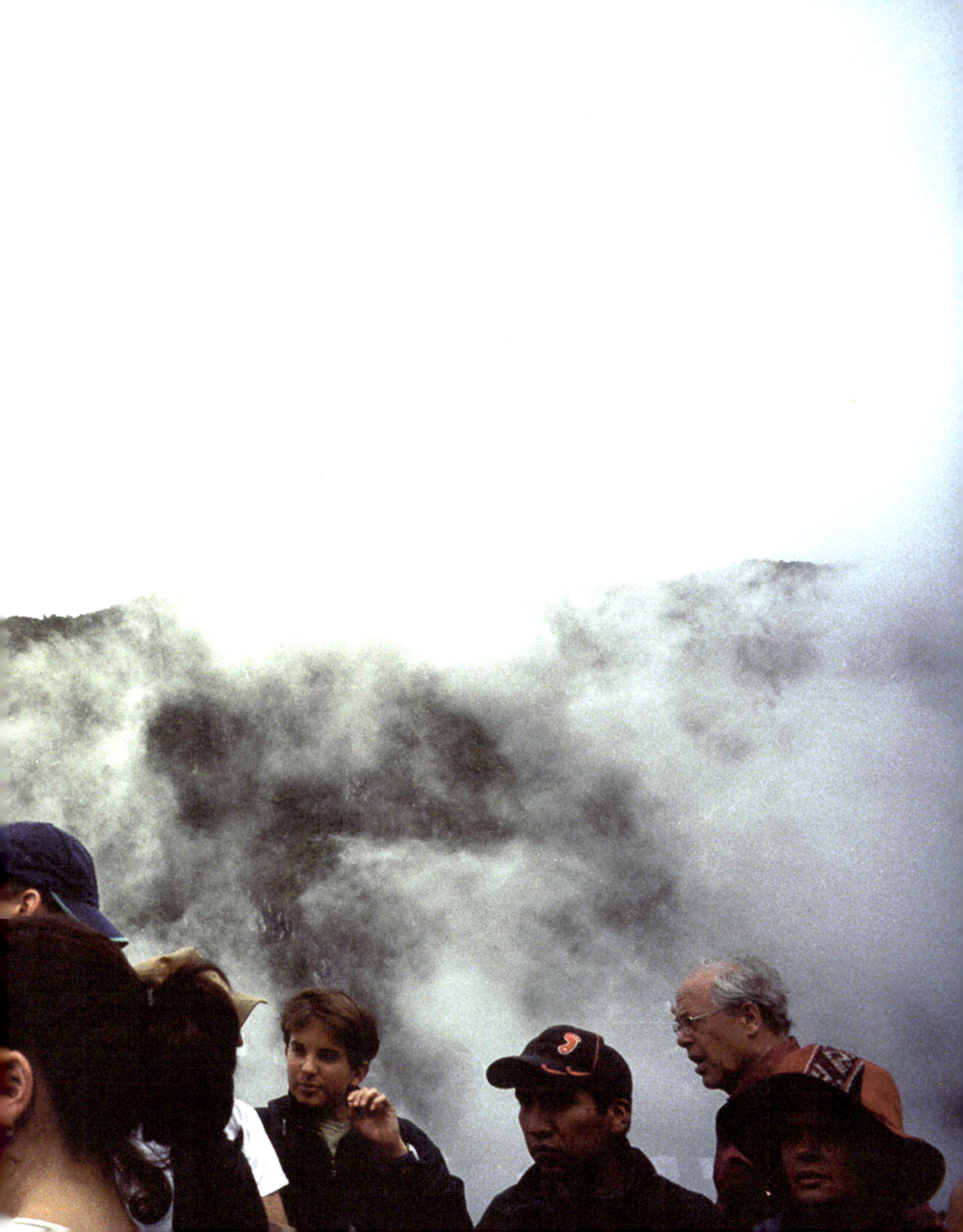

ambiguous and cryptic photographs were, paradoxically, as direct as a snapshot, an aesthetic that was wholeheartedly embraced. This push/pull between the enigmatic and the matter-of-fact occupying the same space was the engine that drove the work of Traeger and The Young Meteors.

Traeger's use of the snapshot aesthetic is beautifully articulated in *Model Tamara Nyman* (*Vogue*, 1963), as realism and fashion share the same stage and the principal player is no longer the model but the interaction of the players within the frame. The image shows one of the many off-center squares in Europe, with Ms. Nyman on the far right, leaning against a very old wall that contrasts nicely with her youth, in a matter-of-fact way, arms at her sides like a kid. On the left, an older man dressed in black, with a top hat for some special occasion, carries a long ceremonial object that looks like an enormous trophy. Near the center, a boy of about twelve looks at the man in black with a very serious air that reminds us that the end of World War II was only 18 years in the past. The left side of the frame is beautifully composed in a traditional manner, and could easily be a Henri Cartier-Bresson from his 1930s period, but the model on the right, smiling contently, creates an extraordinary sense of play—of

fiction entering the scene and creating a sense of stagecraft. The delicate geometry of the space and its local inhabitants beautifully play off the model, as in musical counterpoint.

Another image, from *Elle* magazine (unpublished) in 1962, shows a model sitting in an outdoor cafe, while Traeger shoots from inside through the glass window. The model looks left at someone blocked to us by a wall full of random layers of adverts and text that have been piled one on top of another over time, haphazardly creating an unintentional overlay of diagonals with fragmented text, reminiscent of a cubist paper collage. Another arbitrary element that is used pictorially is the old steam heater under the model that produces a series of vertical lines, like notes, that play off another series of narrow verticals on the window reflections on the opposite side of the frame—creating an extraordinary sense of visual counterpoint. Meanwhile, in the background, a lone male passerby looks on, resigned, hands in pockets—like a poem by Jacques Prévert—the poetics of urban space was never expressed more beautifully.

Aside from Traeger and the Young Meteors in England, there were other photographers at the time who were working with the snapshot

"The boundary between the end of childhood and the beginnings, however rudimentary, of adult life, is vague."

—Denise Levertov

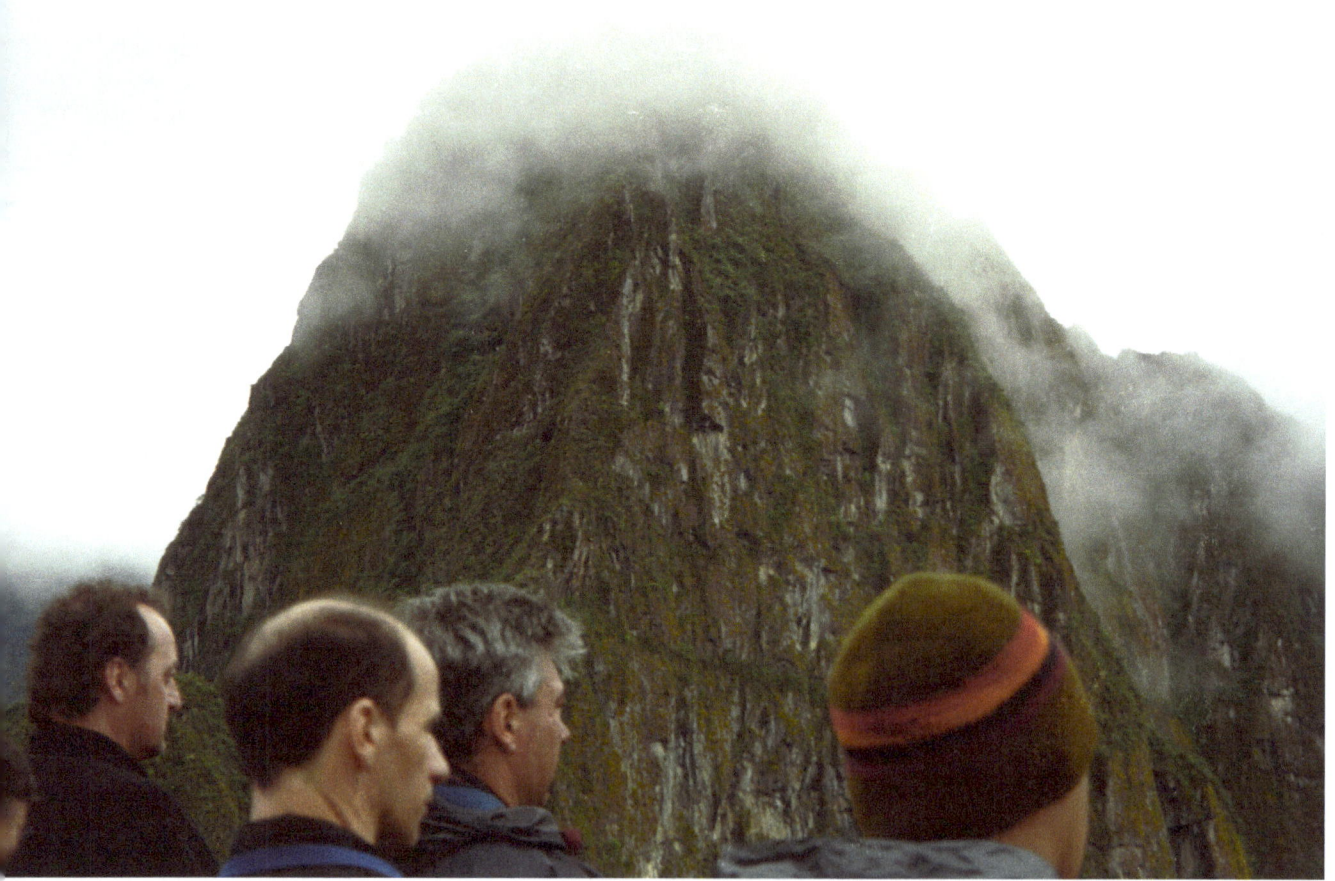

1999 Peru Tourists and Cliff

aesthetic and exploring its possibilities, such as Gordon Parks and Helen Levitt in the United States, Agustín Jiménez in Mexico, Raymond Depardon in France and Ramon Masats in Spain among others. There was also the influence of American post-war action painting with their emphasis on improvisation, emotional integrity, directness and speed, as well as William Klein's influential and ground-breaking book *Life is Good & Good for You in New York*, published in Paris in 1956, and Robert Frank's *The Americans* two years later. Frank worked from an improvisational, emotionally-open foundation, linked more to Beat poetry and jazz than to formal European street photography, that was also an influence. Contingent and fragmentary framing, with cryptic or digressive narrative cues were Frank's strengths. He captured in black and white the evanescent moment beyond Cartier-Bresson's suave, classical balance. After Frank, the French master seemed somewhat affected and cautious. Helen Levitt, another member of the New York School, was also an influence. She immersed herself in a profoundly humanist relationship with her subjects—mostly on the streets of New York. Her images pivot between a casual, almost laconic, framing with highly deliberate juxtapositions that were as formally nuanced as a ballet.

But for many, it was Klein's graphically adventurous, high contrast work that best caught the spirit of the time and place with panache and humor. Klein pioneered a radical open frame that, in opposition to classicism, suggested various conflicting and contrasting realities within the same space—some open and some closed off—some making their entrances and some their exits. The effect was revolutionary as the images suggested that it was possible to capture not only the surfaces of urban life, as had been done in the past, but the experience itself translated into an aesthetic plane of black and white. The liberal use of deep focus allowed Klein to juxtapose not only across the frame, but within the deep space created by his creative use of wide angle lenses and fast film. His use of Kodak Tri-X 600 ASA was normally associated with photojournalists who did not have the time to switch films from interior to exterior or sunny and overcast; subsequently the emphasis was on the film's versatility. The price paid for this wide range of exposures was a high degree of grain. This graininess was derided at the time, at least in art photography, and seen as a sign of photo-journalism, or worse, amateurishness. Klein not only accepted the grain of high-speed film but reveled in it, and emphasized the grain in his printing methods by using high contrast paper and cropping to further increase the grain. Klein influenced several generations of photographers, most famously perhaps the Tokyo-based Daido Moriyama, who would take Klein's urban poetics and push them to the breaking point.

Two other influences on Traeger's work in this European period are Mario Giacomelli and John Cowan. Giacomelli's high contrast black and white pictures, that virtually eliminate mid-tonal greys, were taken primarily in southern Italy where he lived. They are intense and suggestive, with a gravitas that would prove enormously influential to photographers and filmmakers. Giacomelli played with formalism, but was sympathetic to his subjects in a way that was reminiscent of Italian Neorealism, a style that was both realistic and allegorical. His cropping was idiosyncratic and judiciously fragmented, suggesting both the film still and the anthropological fragment. John Cowan was a London-based photographer, somewhat older than the Young Meteors, who was a gifted photographer of movement and dramatic narrative action influenced by genre films. He always employed athletic models who could climb, jump, and hop over a fence. Cowan was himself influenced by Martin Munkácsi, who originated this athletic style in the 1920s, but

while Munkácsi favored the playgrounds of the ultra-rich, Cowan set everything in contemporary London, using the city itself—with its contrasts of class and historical styles—as a stage. Cowan is now perhaps best known as an influence on Michelangelo Antonioni's *Blow-Up* (1966) as he lent technical advice to the director, and it was his loft in Notting Hill that was used as the photographer's studio. Most importantly, it is Cowan's dramatic black and white pictures that graphically captured people in motion, that we see as belonging to the photographer in Antonioni's film, and that come to symbolize the newly liberated freedom from conventions—both social and photographic—that *Blow-Up* explores.

Traeger's London pictures would blend all of these styles and add brilliant saturated color with a sense of giddy, exuberant play. The models often mime a ritualized dance where people play with each other, mimicking the play of children but with adult bodies and an adult sexuality. The two are not separate, as in the American puritan model, wherein one leaves behind the creative play of childhood to assume adult sexuality, responsibilities and ambitions. Rather, the adult and the child are integrated into an organic, conceptually

"The contrasts of movement and stasis, of communication and silence, of closeness and separateness, is beautifully articulated in a shot that seems both carefully planned and completely spontaneous."

coherent whole that is expressed pictorially as play, both formally and in terms of the content. Traeger's magnificent shot of Jill Kennington (Cowan's favorite model) and Donyale Luna running on the beach is one of the great fashion shots of the period. Luna was the first African American model to be featured regularly in fashion magazines, and eventually co-starred in Federico Fellini's *Satyricon* (1969). Her move to London was predicated on her non-marketability in the USA, due to the repercussions of widespread cancellation of subscriptions once she appeared on a six page spread in *Harper's Bazaar* (1965) shot by Richard Avedon. In London, she rebooted her career, working regularly for *Vogue,* who only published her pictures in the European market. Despite her incredible otherworldly appearance—like some form of advanced human being—she was a Detroit girl and must have bonded with Traeger, as the two young Americans were on the loose in London in the decade that would culturally define the rest of the century and beyond.

What makes the image so uniquely Traeger's is that he has taken Cowan's ideas regarding movement within the shot, and Klein's open frame to the next level. The models are literally escaping the frame, Kennington from the top

and Luna from the bottom, as if the camera frame simply could not contain them—they are captured in-media-res just before escaping altogether. This use of the space outside of the frame is cinematic and the influence of films on all of the Young Meteors is clearly evident— more so on the younger emerging talent like Traeger. The other Young Meteors, even Bailey, were still tied, however tentatively, to the traditions of portraiture established by masters like Felix Nadar in the 19th Century. It is Traeger, and the following generation, who would move away from that tradition to a more contemporary cinematic approach.

Traeger's portraiture adopted the improvisational method, embracing the snapshot aesthetic that the Young Meteors also took on. Yet, while his work suggests the casualness and "arbitrary" framing of snapshots, the pictures have a graphic sophistication in their interplay of forms, flattened by the use of a long lens, far beyond the aesthetics of the snapshot. A good example is the 1967 double portrait of Britt Ekland and Peter Sellers. They were at the time enormously successful film stars, each with their own career—equals in every sense and a model couple for the new generation coming of age in the sixties. Sellers talks on a, then very rare, car phone, while Ekland exits the vehicle

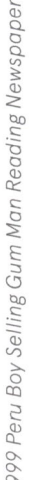

1999 Peru Boy Selling Gum Man Reading Newspaper

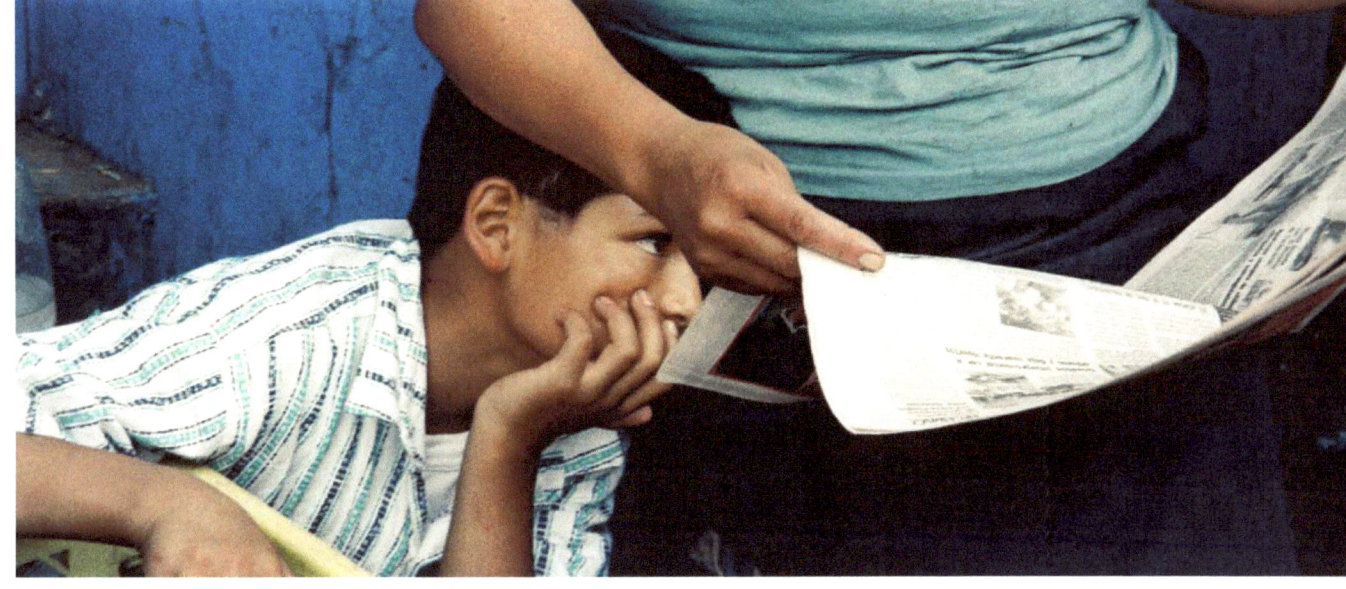

"A sensibility like Traeger's, fascinated by paradox, cannot help but see comedy and tragedy, historical locations and everyday life, as an organic whole."

to the right. The two are framed within the frame of the car window, while her hair, blown by the wind, creates another frame for her face—the hair also links up with Seller's phone uniting the two. While that might seem obvious since they were then a couple, it is clear that the two are occupying very different psychological spaces despite their proximity.

Does this hint at the separation soon to follow? Sellers sits calmly and looks to his left, deep in the middle of a conversation, while Ekland, in the midst of casually moving off, looks up at something outside the frame, opening up the image to what lies beyond. The contrasts of movement and stasis, of communication and silence, of closeness and separateness, is beautifully articulated in a shot that seems both carefully planned and completely spontaneous.

While all of the Young Meteors photographed the supermodel Twiggy—to the delight of young and old—she is perhaps the collaborator that is most closely tied to Traeger's successful fashion work. The sense of spontaneous play that was his trademark style was pushed to new heights with Twiggy, perhaps because of her short, close-cropped hair and skinny frame, which sometimes made her resemble

an adult/child. Traeger used that aspect of her physical beauty and temperament in his shot at Battersea Park from 1967. Twiggy, mouth fully open, perhaps screaming in delight, sits astride a mini bike on a dirt road, perfectly caught between childhood and adulthood—the two seem to merge and create a sense of extraordinary play. This giddy delight is both very much of its time, but also transcends it to state a philosophical case for the permanence of childhood, at least as a conceptual space that is more about the experience of childhood as an idea that can be expressed through the body by an adult. It is a phenomenological position, but to understand how philosophy works in a pictorial sense we need to look at Traeger's earlier work.

Traeger's Roman pictures from 1962 are in effect his portfolio by which he secured the fashion work of the mid-sixties. The Roman images consistently juxtapose a graphically imposing foreground, often in silhouette, with a distinct but fragmented background. The long focal length lens flattens foreground and background that then work dramatically together—as in musical counterpoint—by playing interlocking shapes one against the other. Organic shapes mirror man-made surfaces; negative spaces come forward and foregrounds recede; the archaic is juxtaposed with the contemporary; Christian iconography is played off against Marxist symbols; people in dramatic movement play off against solid, stationary masses.

In short, the work is about these very urban paradoxes. The work in many ways resembles the films of the French New Wave—Godard's *Breathless* (1960), Truffaut's *The 400 Blows* (1959), Agnès Varda's *Cleo From 5 to 7* (1962) and Éric Rohmer's *The Bakery Girl of Monceau* (1963) are Traeger's true contemporaries. The French New Wave traveled across the channel in the late fifties and early sixties and had a profound influence on British filmmakers and photographers. The films display what (with apologies to Harold Bloom) we might call "the exuberance of influence." It is the kind of work that resists conceptual summarizing truths in favor of a fragmented collage aesthetic. It should not come as a surprise that Traeger also made collages and even a comic strip using photographs and hand painted balloons with dialog. A sensibility like Traeger's, fascinated by paradox, cannot help but see comedy and tragedy, historical locations and everyday life, as an organic whole. In a sense this viewpoint makes every moment precious since it is preordained that it must, like everything else,

pass into oblivion or into some cosmological sense of time that we can perhaps never understand. Traeger was an artist fascinated by the complex, organic minutiae of the quotidian at the expense of any theory that might explain reality by fitting it into an organized system of knowledge. This is precisely where he departed, literally and figuratively, from his teachers, still tied to the conceptual tableaus of advertising and fine art then in vogue.

Finally, Traeger's pictures are eloquent about what Proust called the "tyranny of the particular." This was Proust's term for the sensual stimulation of direct experience that overwhelmed Proust because he made himself be completely open to it—most people don't for the obvious reason that to do so requires a cork-lined room to then be able to retire to. That "tyranny of the particular" that so disturbed Proust haunts Traeger's images. The long lens has flattened and compressed not only space but also time. A picture of a child playing against the light falling on the side of St. Peter's Cathedral has the soccer ball and the architecture playing against each other and making connections, and we understand that it's Traeger playing as well—and he is asking us to come and play with him. It is as if the time between childhood and adulthood were not only suspended but that it had become a space that one can see and hold in one's hands. That's the thing that Traeger found with his camera in Italy, and he never forgot it—and that is why his photography suggests phenomenology but manages to transcend it as a concept. He accomplishes this by grounding the work in the reality of his own time, allowing the non-sequitur and the exception space to breathe. It should go without saying that fine art photography, as well as advertising—the two sides of the same coin—are conceptually-based so reality is merely there, if at all, simply as window dressing, or worse, as a backdrop to a piece of theater. Traeger understood in his work how the present tense of photography also contains traces of the past and the future, but that this cannot be interpolated—rather, it must be discovered in the world at large. To paraphrase an old saying, "One need not believe in miracles to experience them, but one must be present." Traeger only had a few years as a working photographer, but he was present, and with his camera he allows us a glimpse into that miracle. In that sense, the images can't help but be an invitation to a life of engagement, of exchange, of the senses. The tyranny of the particular—or perhaps more to the point, the delight of the particular—has not been better served since.

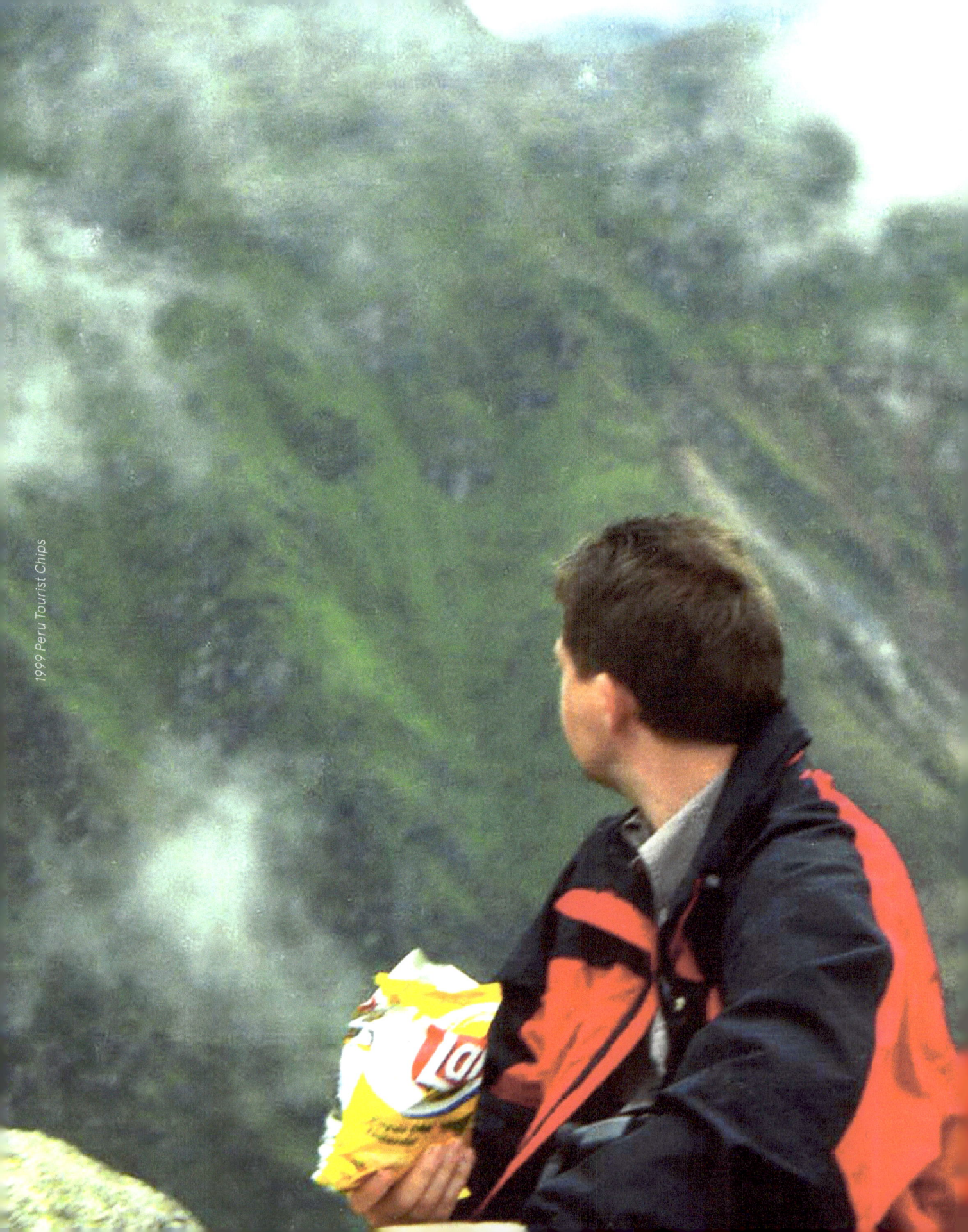

1999 Peru Tourist Chips

El Laberinto Dos

Mark von Schlegell

"And does the author," Don Quixote asked, "by any chance promise a second part?"

"Yes, he does," Sansón replied, "but he says he hasn't found it and doesn't know who's got it, so we can't tell whether it'll come out or not—and both because of this and because some people are saying, 'What's already been written about Don Quixote is quite enough,' there are doubts about the originality of this part..."

—Miguel de Cervantes, *Don Quixote*

I'd read and published some of his essays in a zine. I had always thought of him as a Californian, but it was in Mexico City where I first met George Porcari face to face. V. and I took a comfortable enough hotel room in the historical district for what amounted to 35 dollars a day. Was it my first trip to Mexico City? I don't think so. When a crowd of V.'s friends from California (only one or two I'd met before) turned up, I spotted George right away as if he was Godard.

Unfortunately, I had to deny his request to sleep on the floor of our cheap hotel room. I simply said "Absolutely no way. You can't sleep here, George."

I had my reasons.

There was something I spotted right away, or I tell myself now after all that has happened in between (Paris '68, for instance) as something I might specifically recognize. A single, almost hygienic, gaze out from the paradoxical center of a fluidity of multiplicitous points-of-view. By almost hygienic, I hope to call attention to the feral nature of what remains, the *hyenic*, proven, self-reliant determination of the laughing eye. It survives now in this revolution. It is not to suggest Porcari is anything but hygienic and that's why I thought of it. Porcari is usually quite immaculate—especially when the niceties have been abandoned. So on our first meeting, when I turned him away, he chuckled and bowed. Presenting an immaculate grin in the face of apocalypse, he withdrew.

Looking back, I seem to see Porcari in characteristic blazer and white shirt, spectacled, arms and legs outstretched, spider-like against the

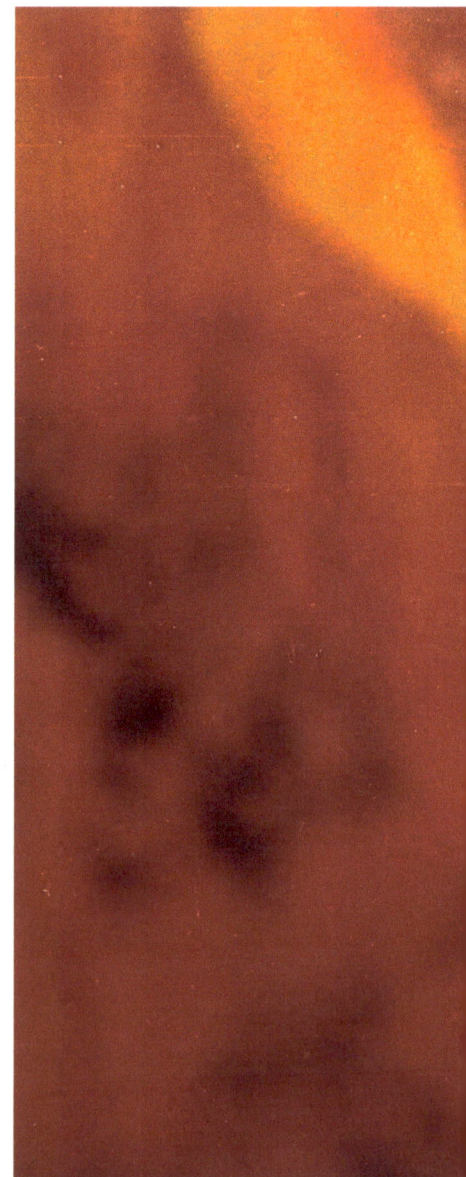

2002 Mark von Schlegell Venice

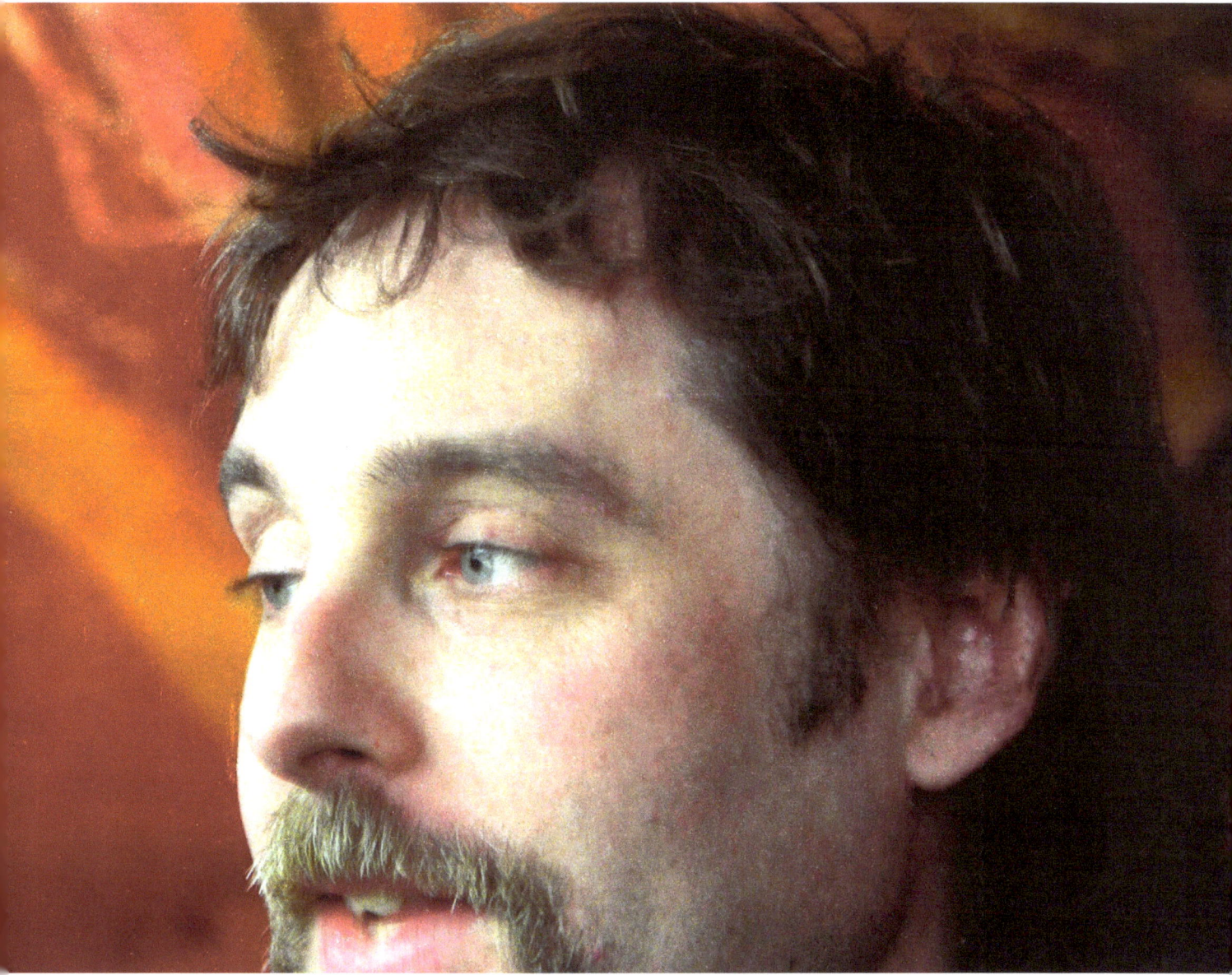

entire visible sphere of the DF. He's infinitely tiled, hand-to-hand, head-to-head, foot-to-foot, like the motif in an Escher print. Porcari's lifelong distaste for Escher (an artist librarian-ship forces him into promulgating) suitably ironizes that image. The man of tastes, the very subject in all its delectable essence, forgoing to paint everyday life at all—rather content to allow it to paint only Porcari repeatedly on the distant film surface of an impossible light-cone. F Heidegger anyway. We prefer the true documentary real of immediate revelation. Porcari's films often have the opposite effect on me as those of Godard—they wake me up. If I go on to dream, it's with the sense that my dreams are units of exchange in a capitalist labyrinth where the limits of freedom are exactly the same as the dimensions of Porcari's library (taking into account its film collection) or sprawling metropolitan Los Angeles of a million other stories.

Unable to shut out the stamping-out of the paperback revolution in The House of Fiction (1987-2000), I wake in vain, tears in my eyes again.

Does the capturing and preserving of total alienation paradoxically preserve the geist of what the past really was? Porcari's shots of tourists in Machu Picchu, Peru tread closely to satire. Yet they have famously revealed secrets of the past that certain authorities deemed unsuitable for public distribution. Because the artist chose to focus neither on the UFO nor on the pyramid, but on a freshly opened bag of potato chips in the hands of a tourist, the pictures have escaped censorship to this day. How strange to remember that the past was always as pure as a just-breathing crisp after the first fragrant pop of the plastic bag. In the seventies, Porcari's pictures reverse the soon-to-be-retro into its surface lie—ovoid disks over gas pads, browns and polyesters outlining an eternal adolescence, inner illumination making splendid a modernist proto-ruin. The past reaches out full of the commodity's first most joyous penetration. It moves the heart as a kind of injustice that that was as new as now. What was I then, I think. A child? Certain airs and fact come to me with a new immediacy, as if I had been in fact then an adult after all, and simply failed to understand it as I do now. The unfairness of human time...

After chilaquiles, the next I saw him, Porcari walked swiftly. A trench coat wrapped his quiet step into the emerging folds of the mysterious city. Not quite the man of the crowd, he could have been anyone potentially able to be alienated by it. I had thought it was night, but was surprised to find when he turned the corner and I followed onto Calle Donceles, that it was morning. Illumination shone from ranks of dark-doored bookstores, stacked with what was to me my first glances of the enormous profusion of a literary past unknown to me (more copies of the *Quixote* alone than there would be volumes in Porcari's library when I came to work there). I found Porcari picking through cut-rate utopias outside a used bookstore called The Labyrinth. Perhaps I told myself it was my first night in Mexico City and it was somehow appropriate that it would be in fact a morning. I don't remember. It was the books that took my attention. And so only now it dawns: Porcari had indeed spent the night in the hotel room.

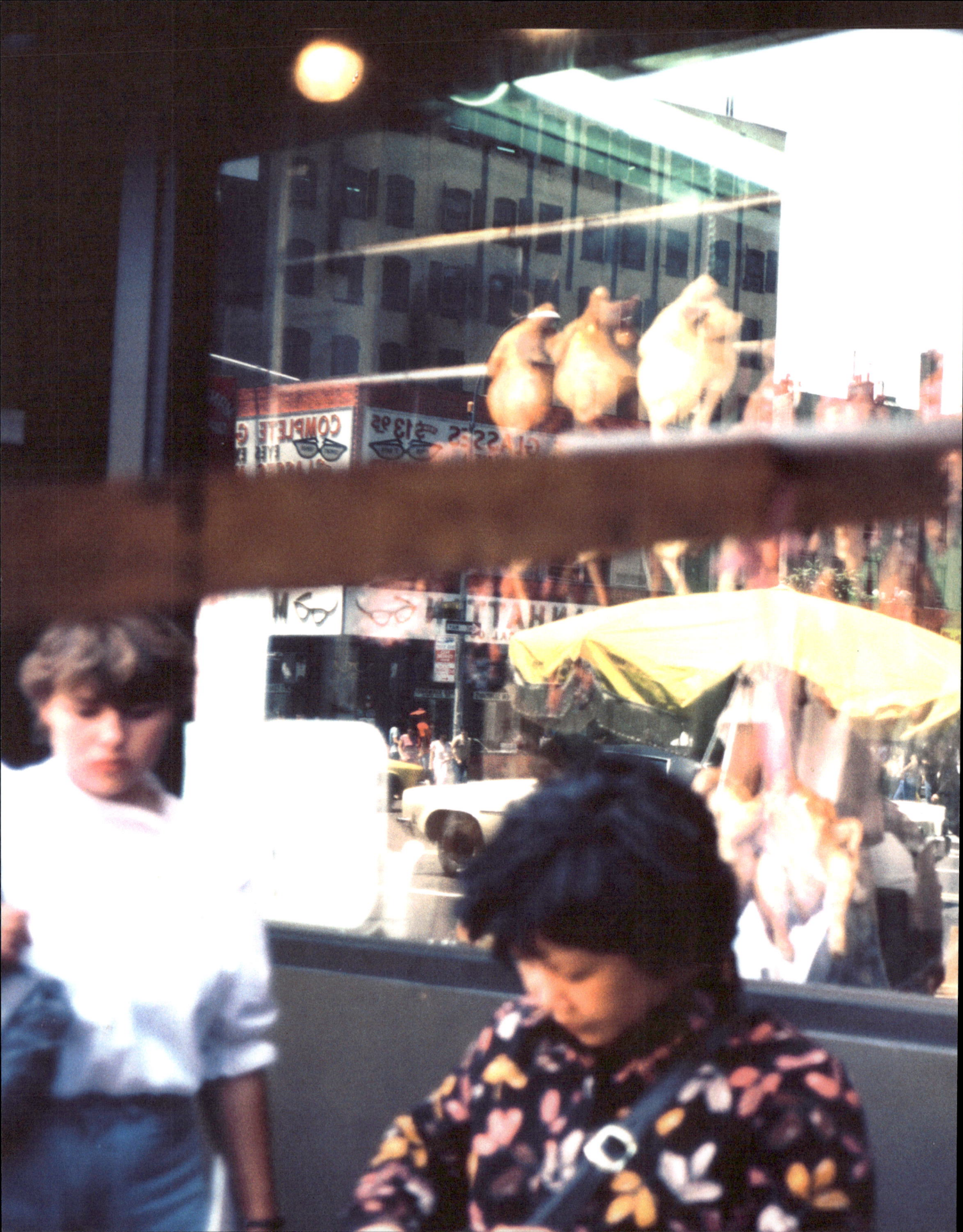

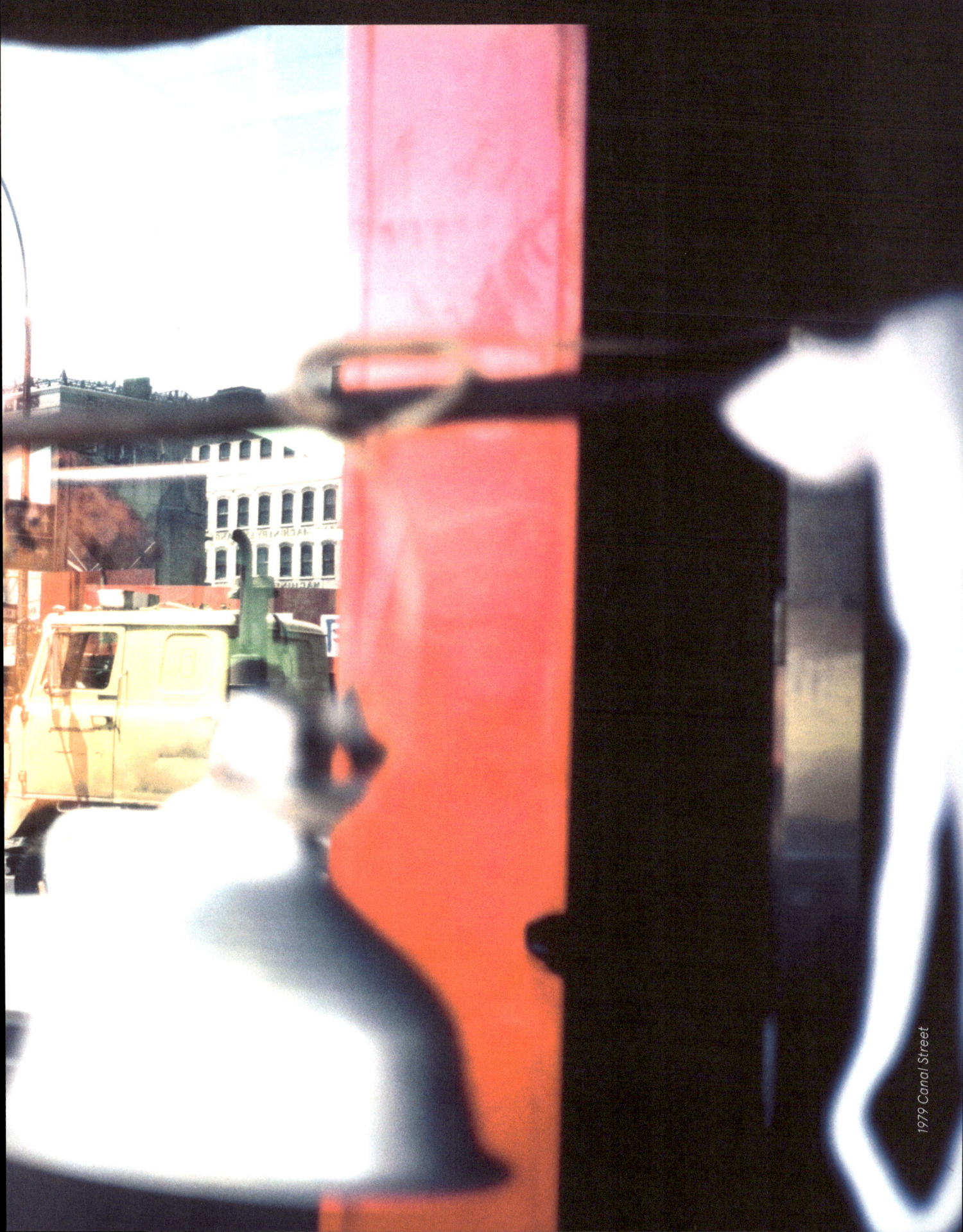

1979 Canal Street

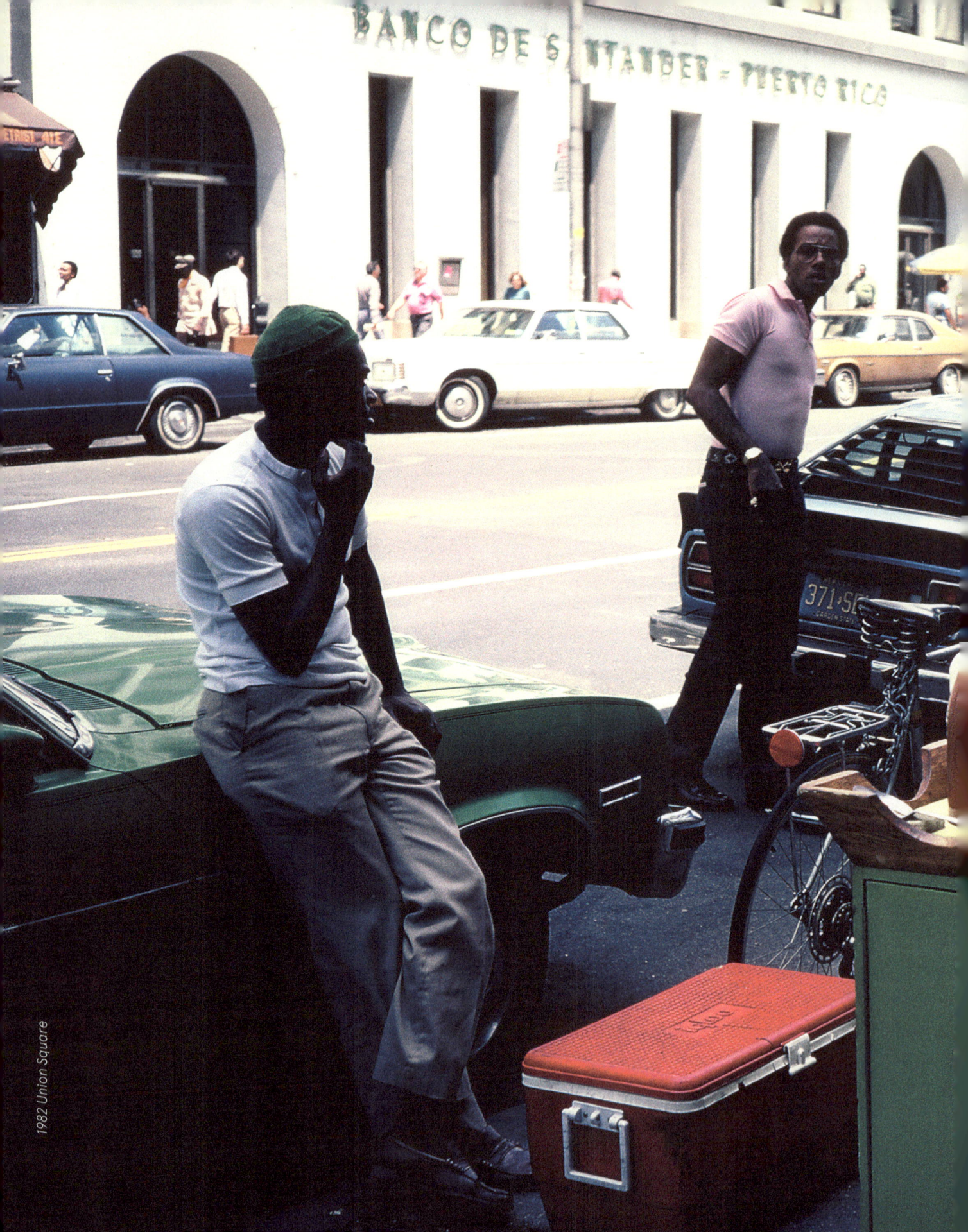

1982 Union Square

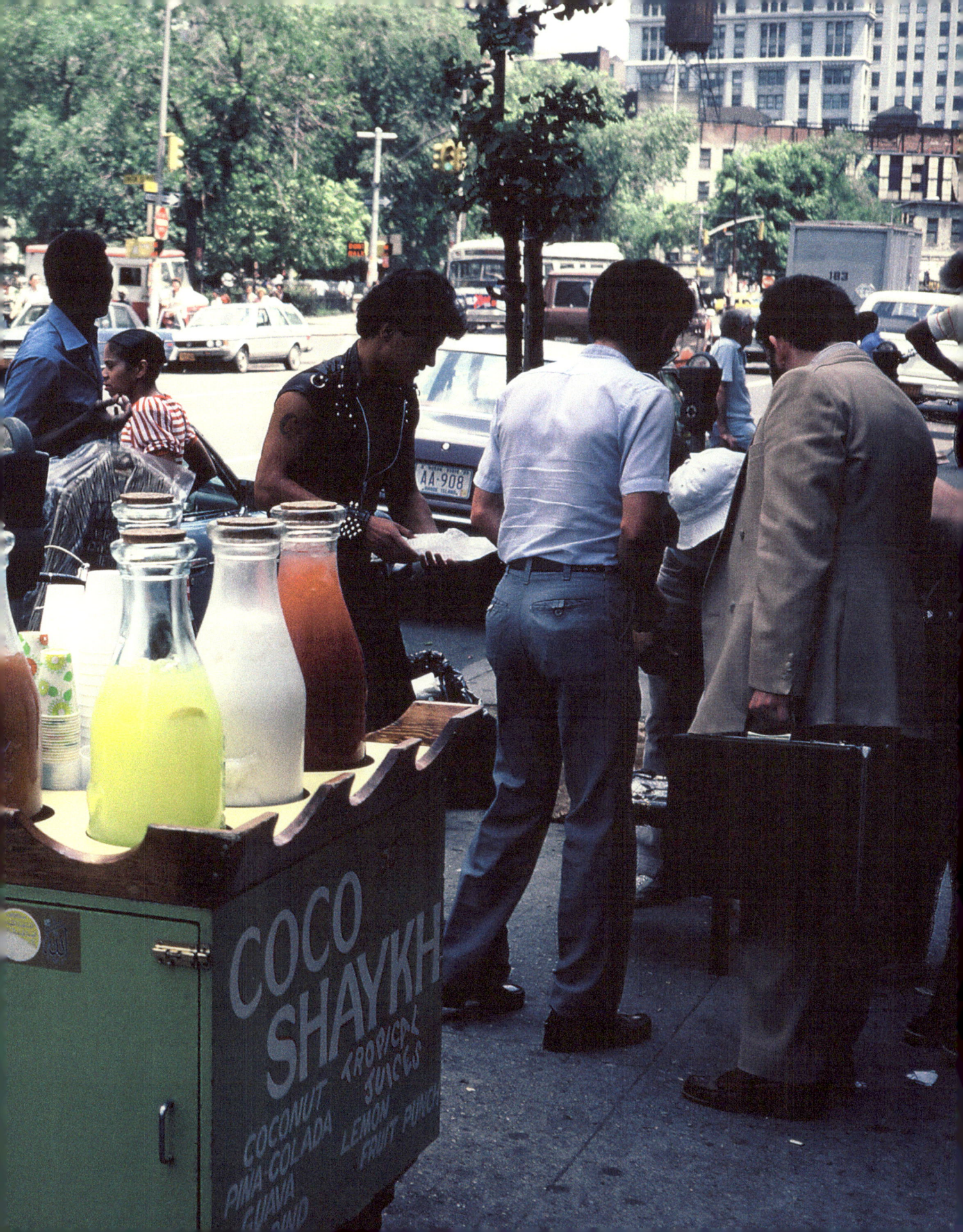

COCO
SHAYKH
COCONUT TROPICAL
PINA COLADA JUICES
GUAVA LEMON
RIND FRUIT PUNCH

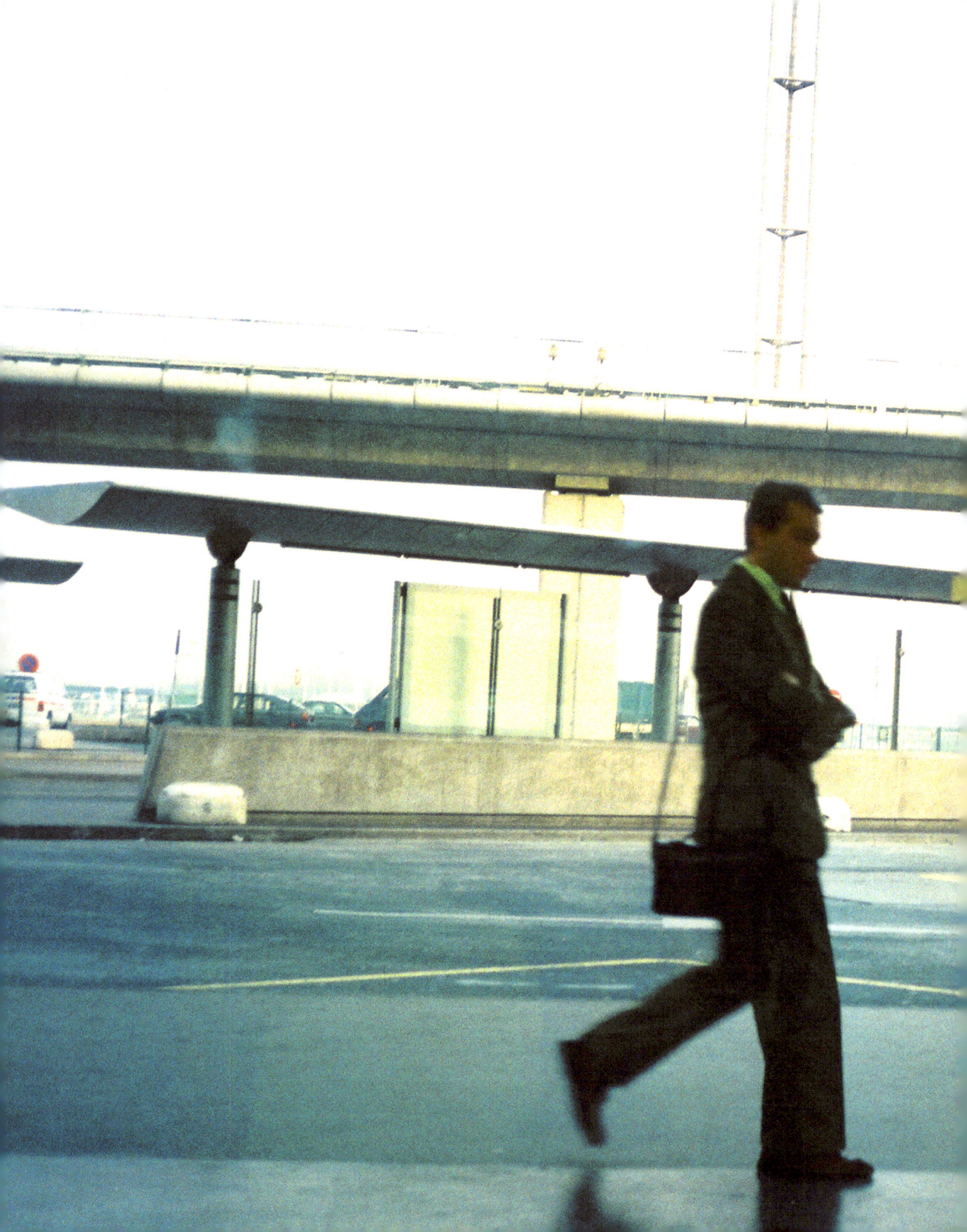

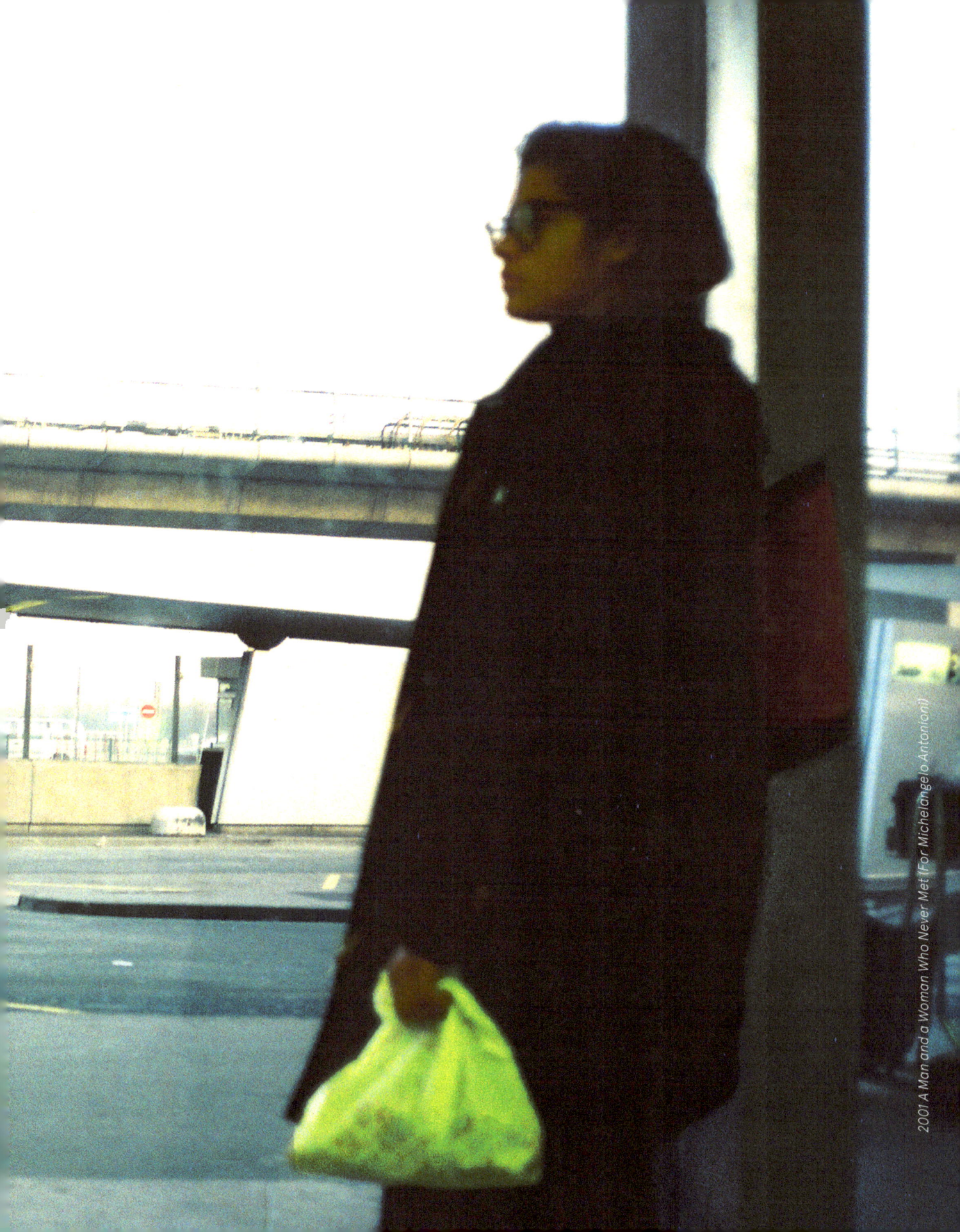

2001 A Man and a Woman Who Never Met (For Michelangelo Antonioni)

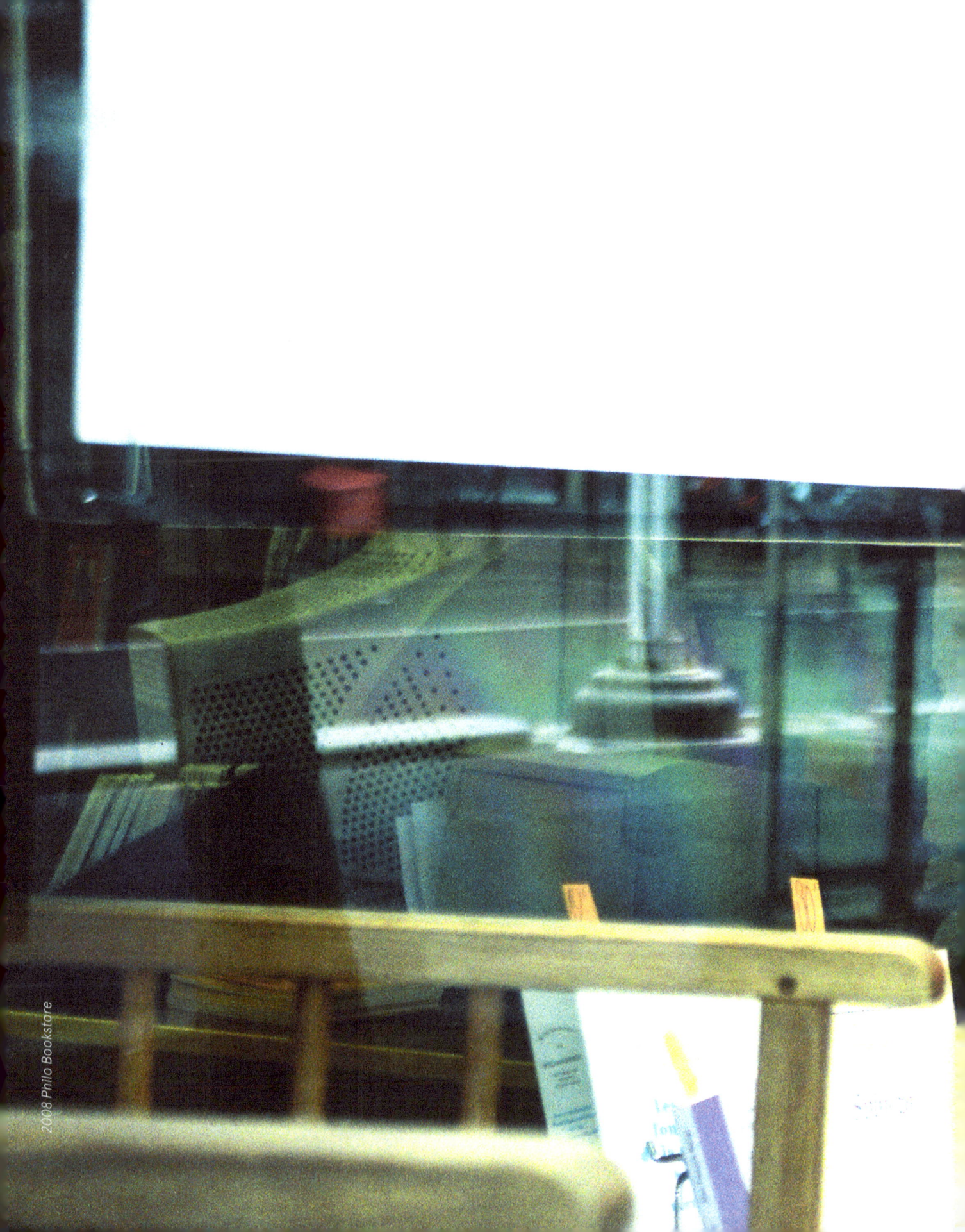

2008 Philo Bookstore

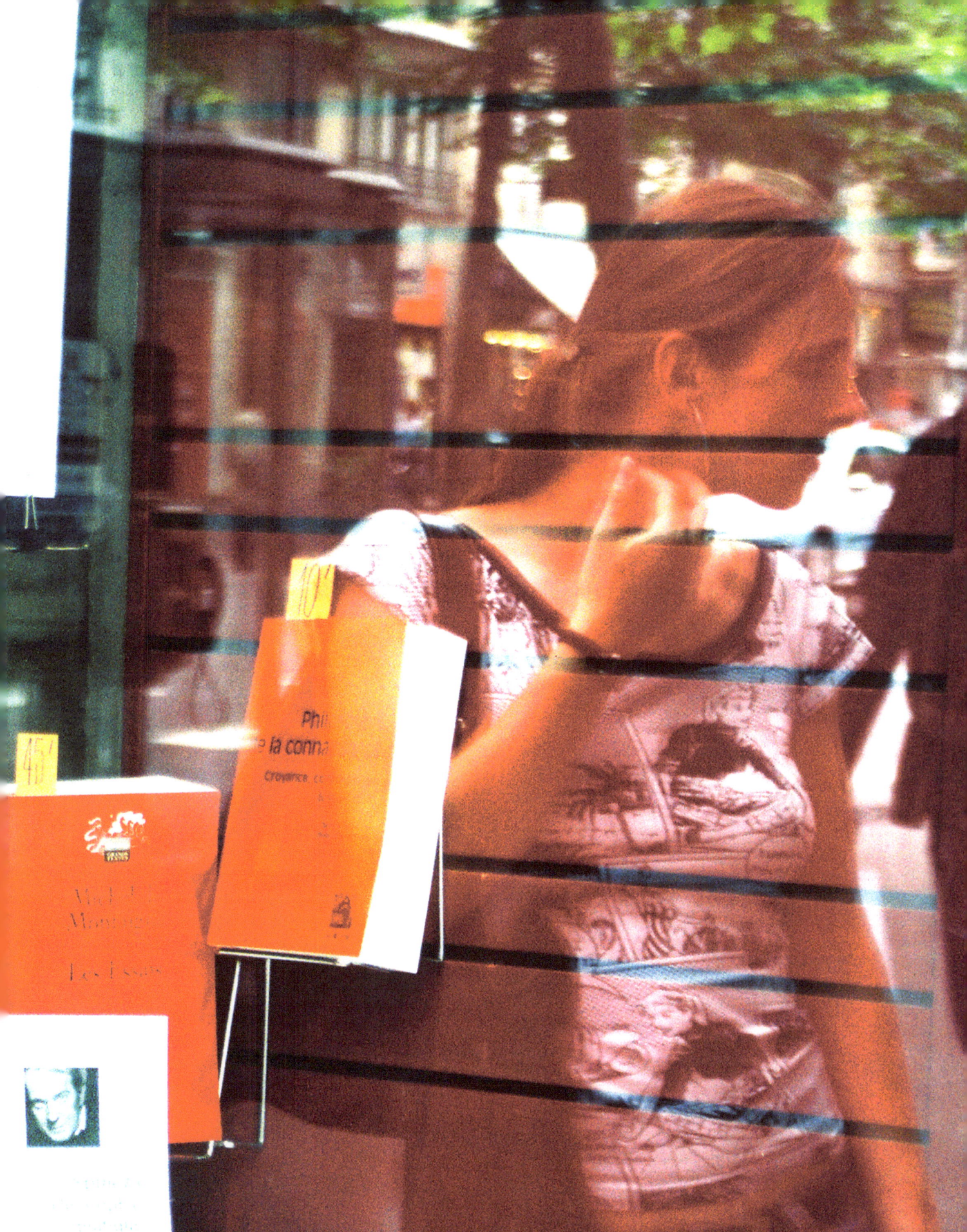

Greetings

From

LA

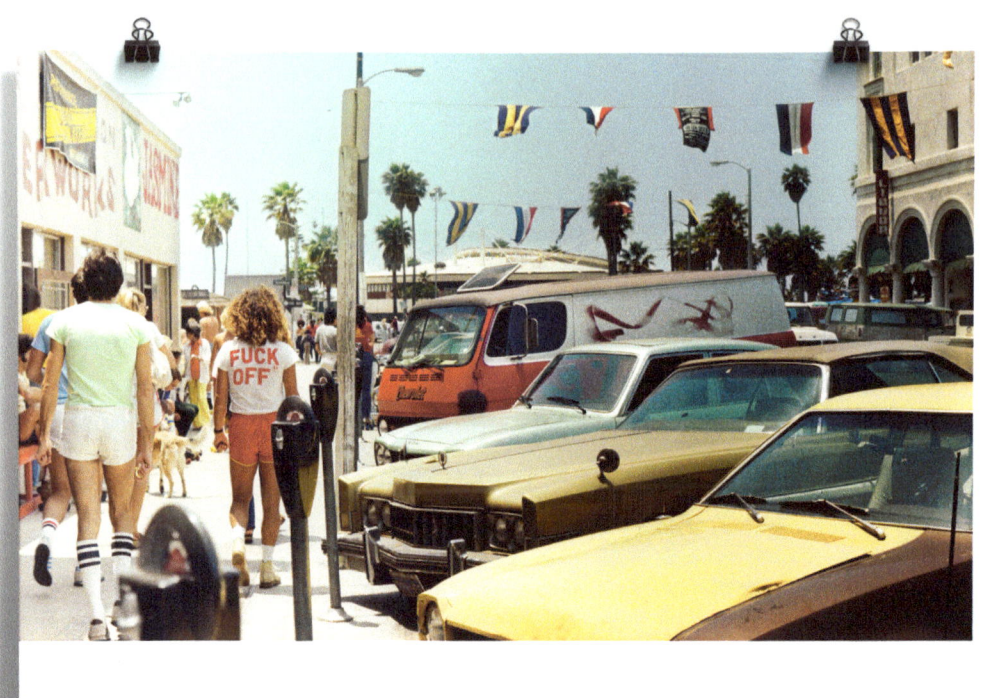

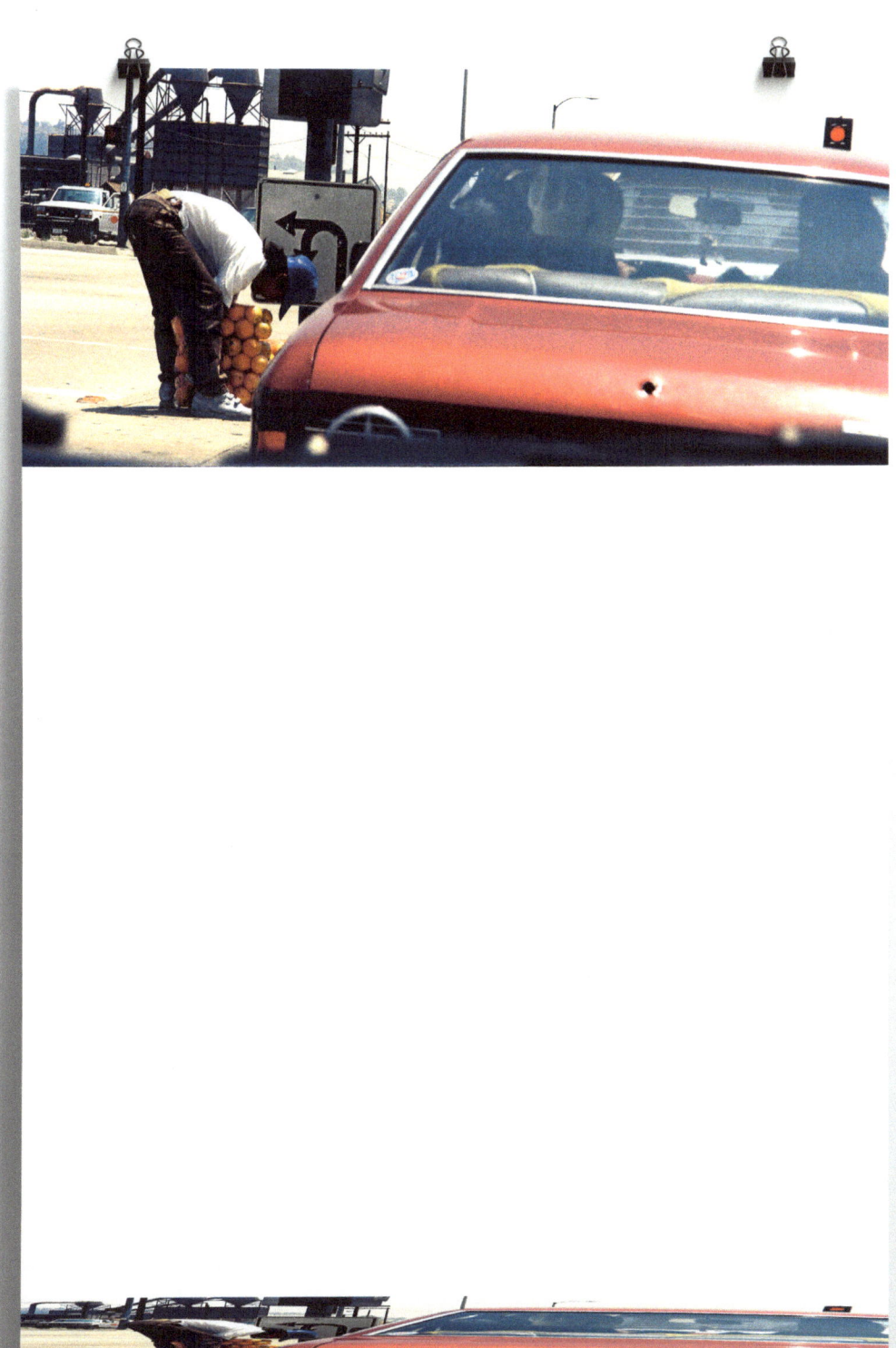

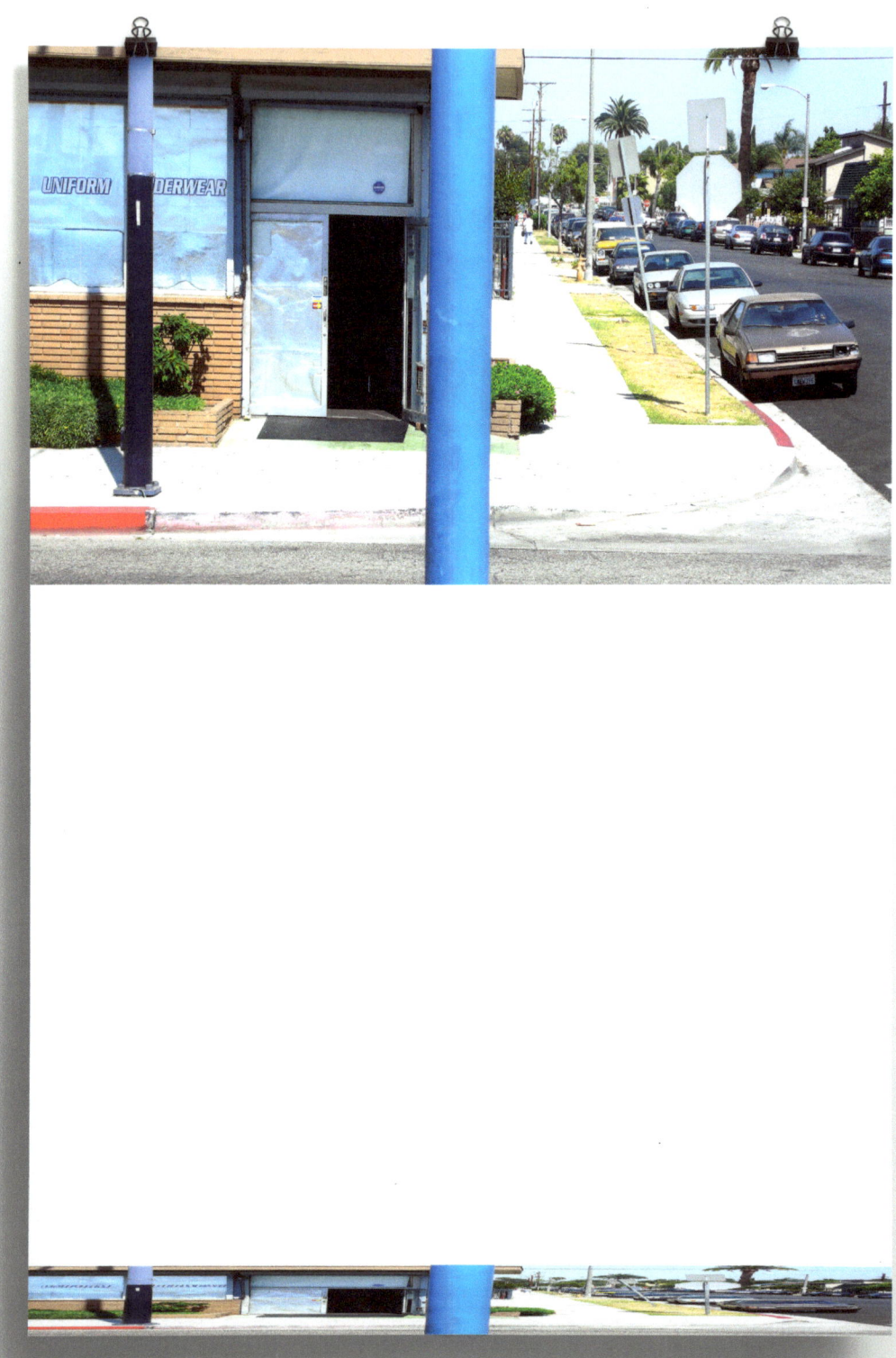

GFLA Long Beach 2006
32 x 46 in

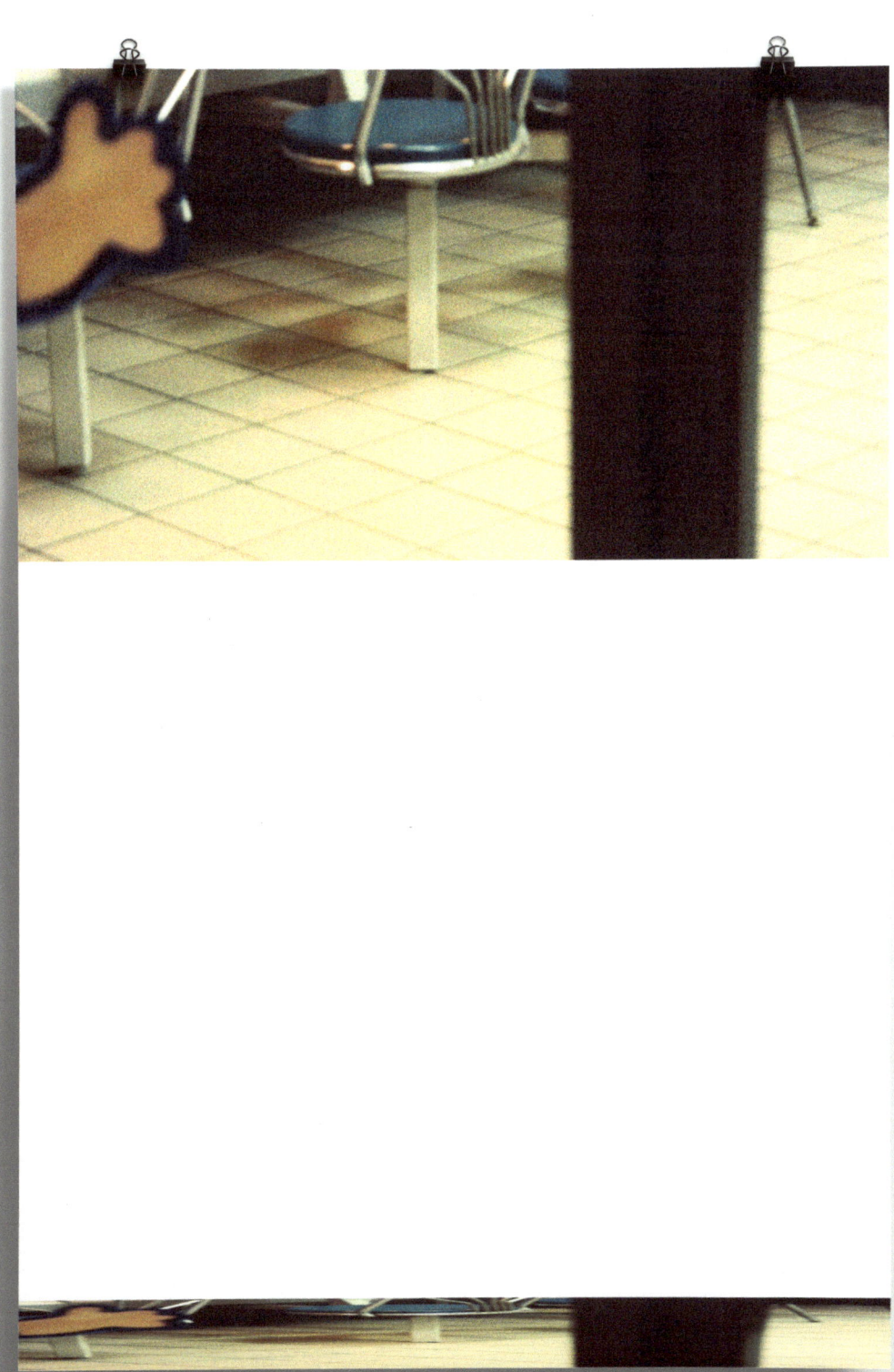

GFLA Melrose 1995
32 x 46 in

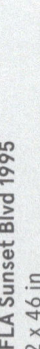

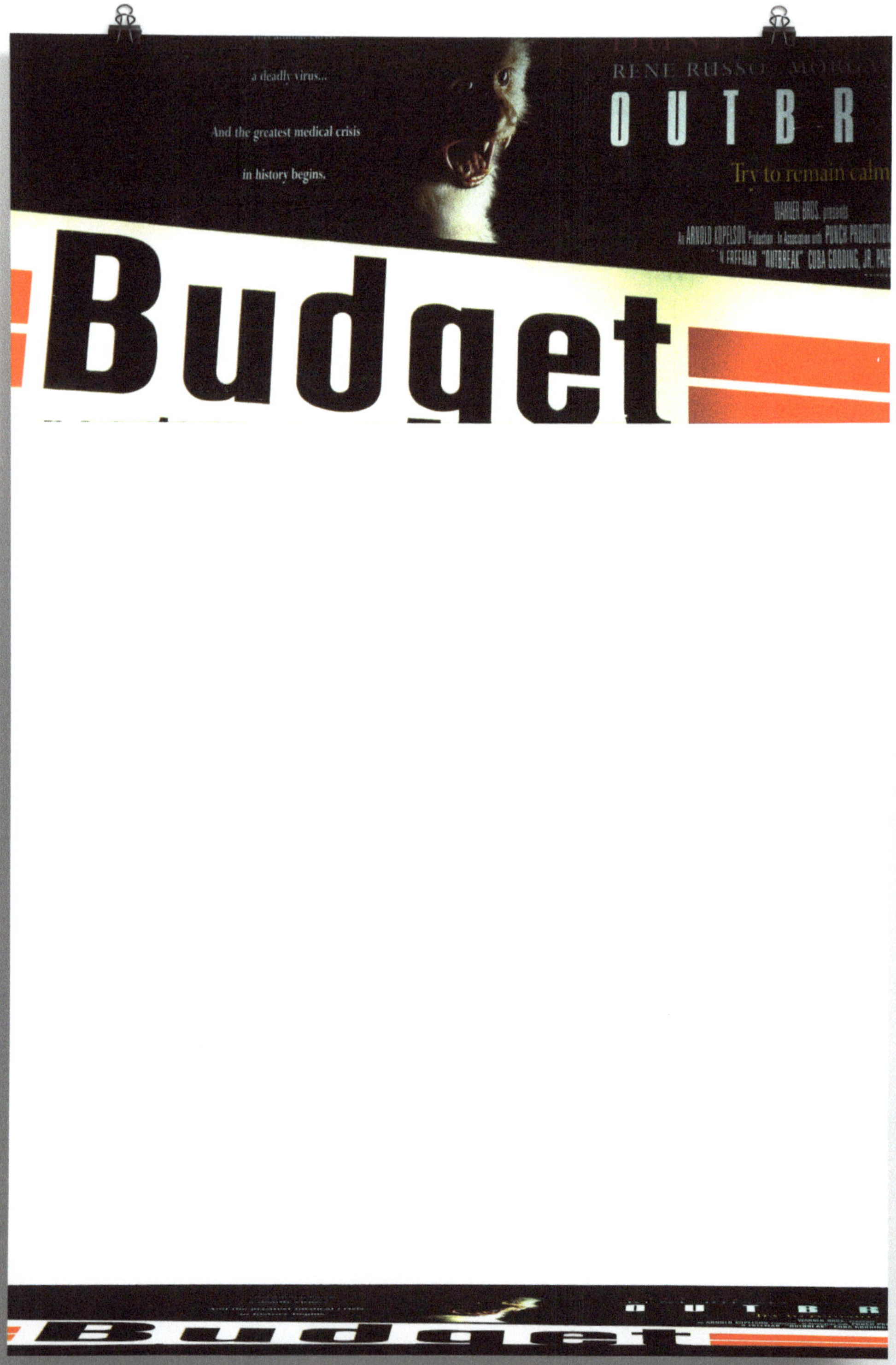

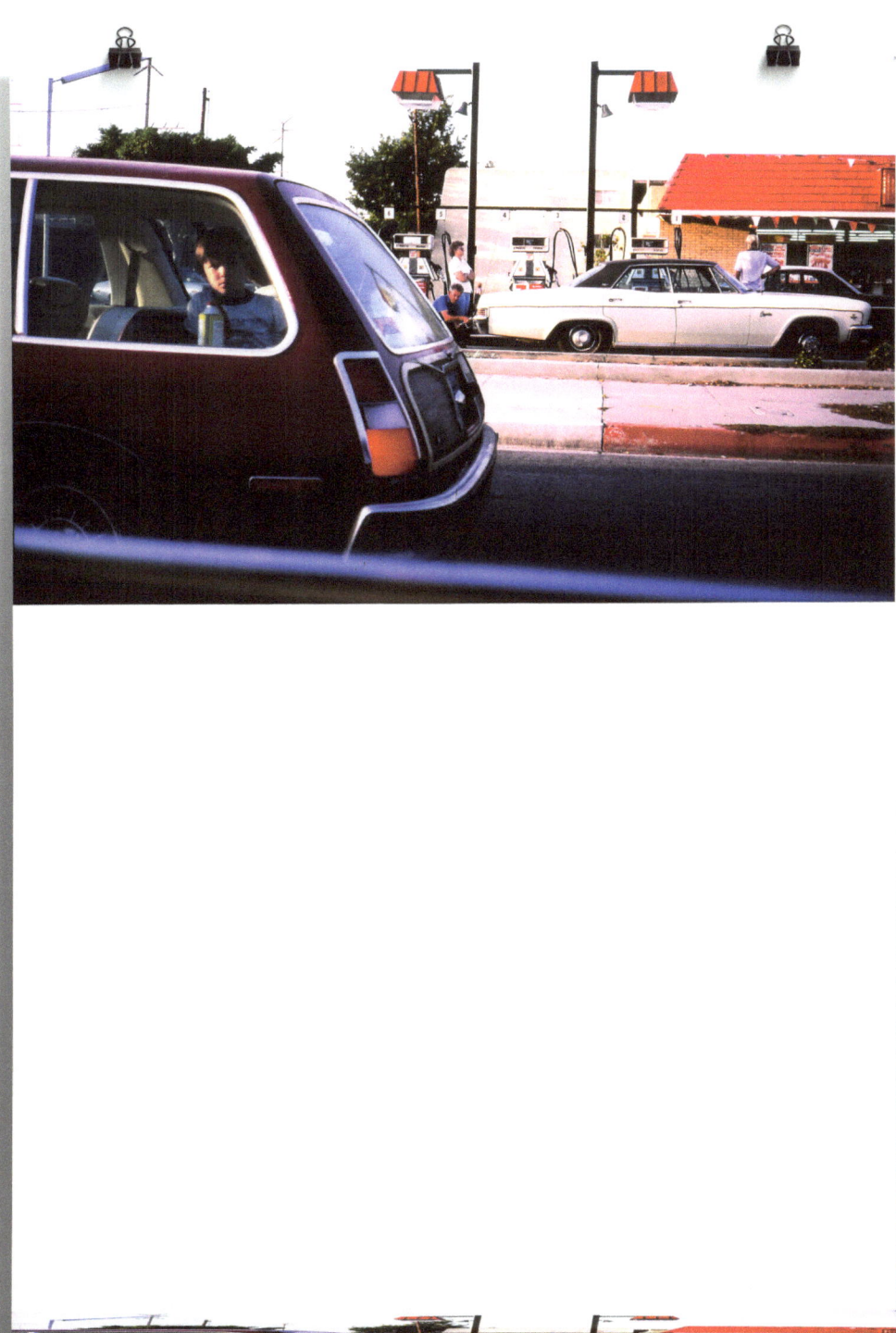

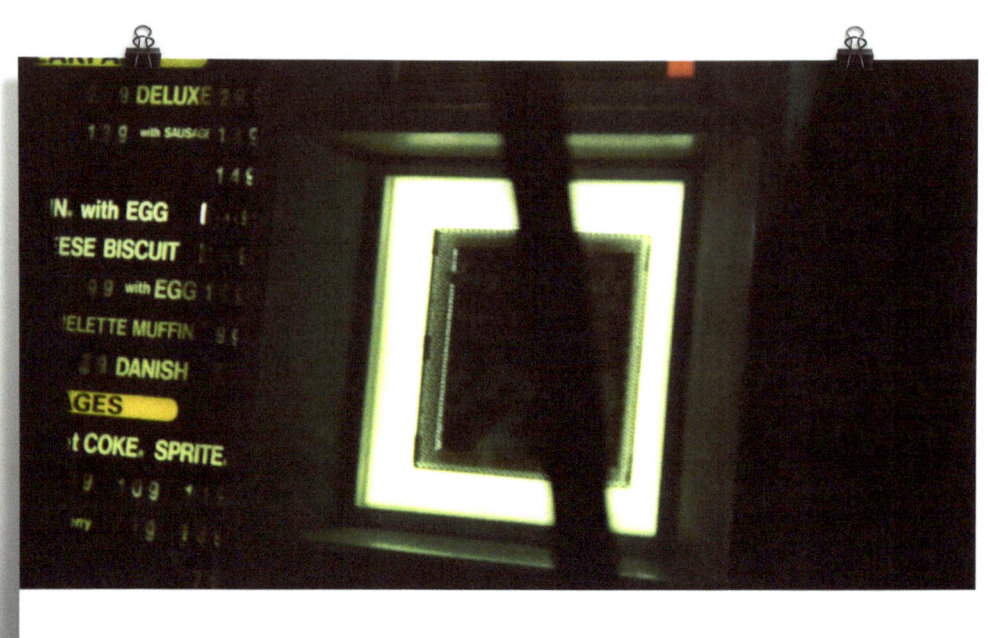

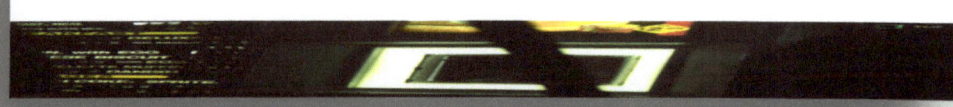

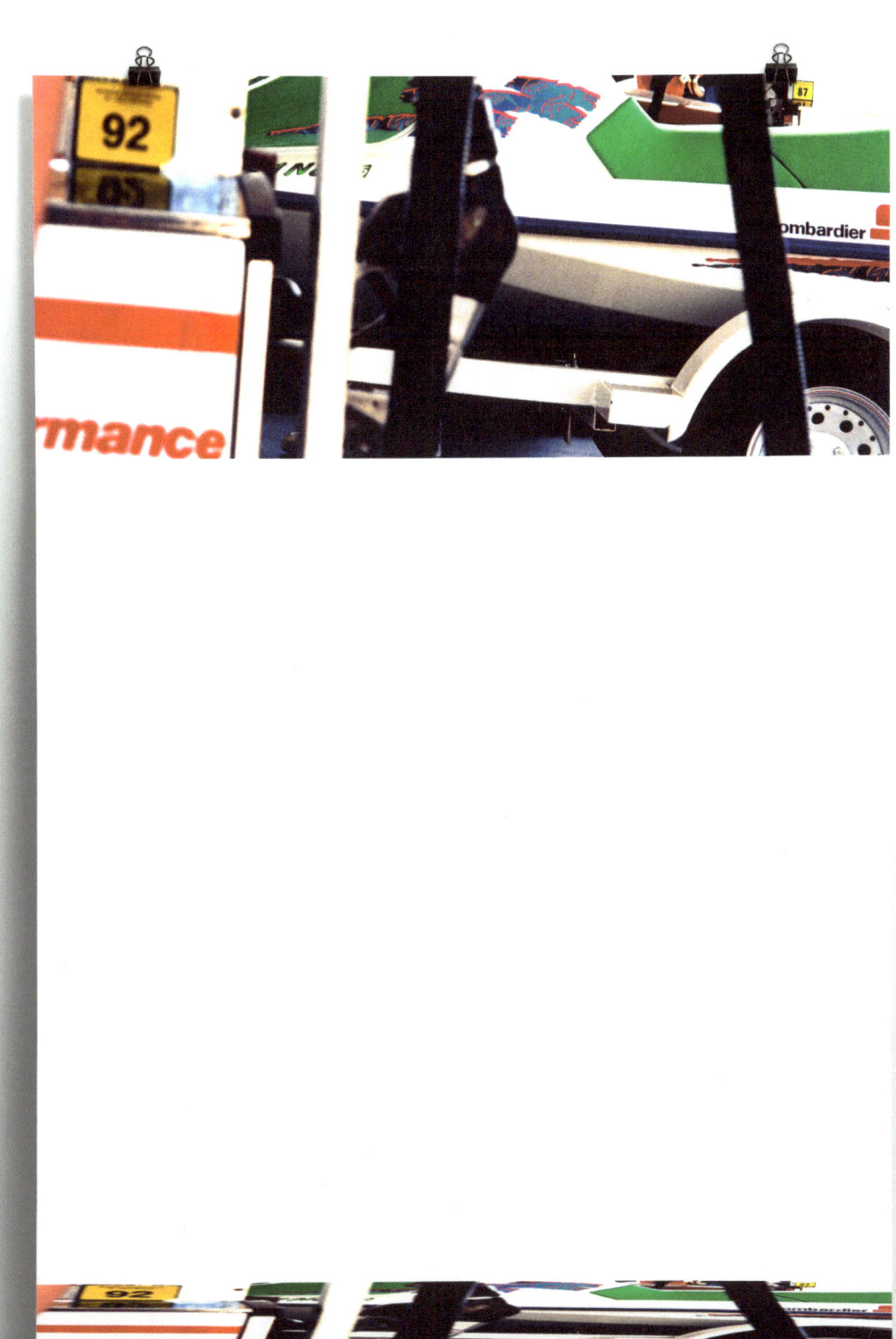

GFLA Redondo Beach 1995
32 x 46 in

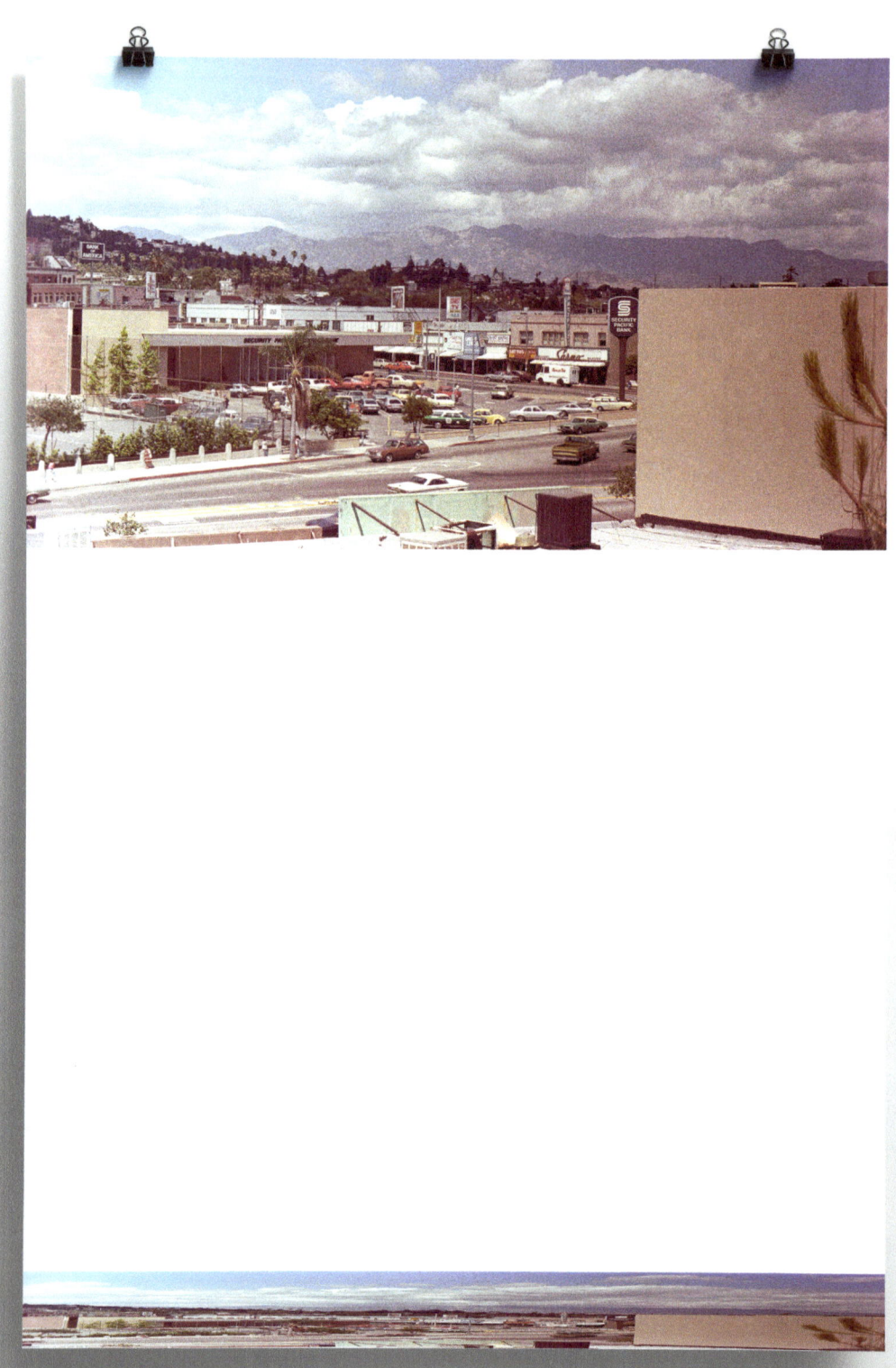

GFLA Los Feliz 1979
32 x 46 in

118

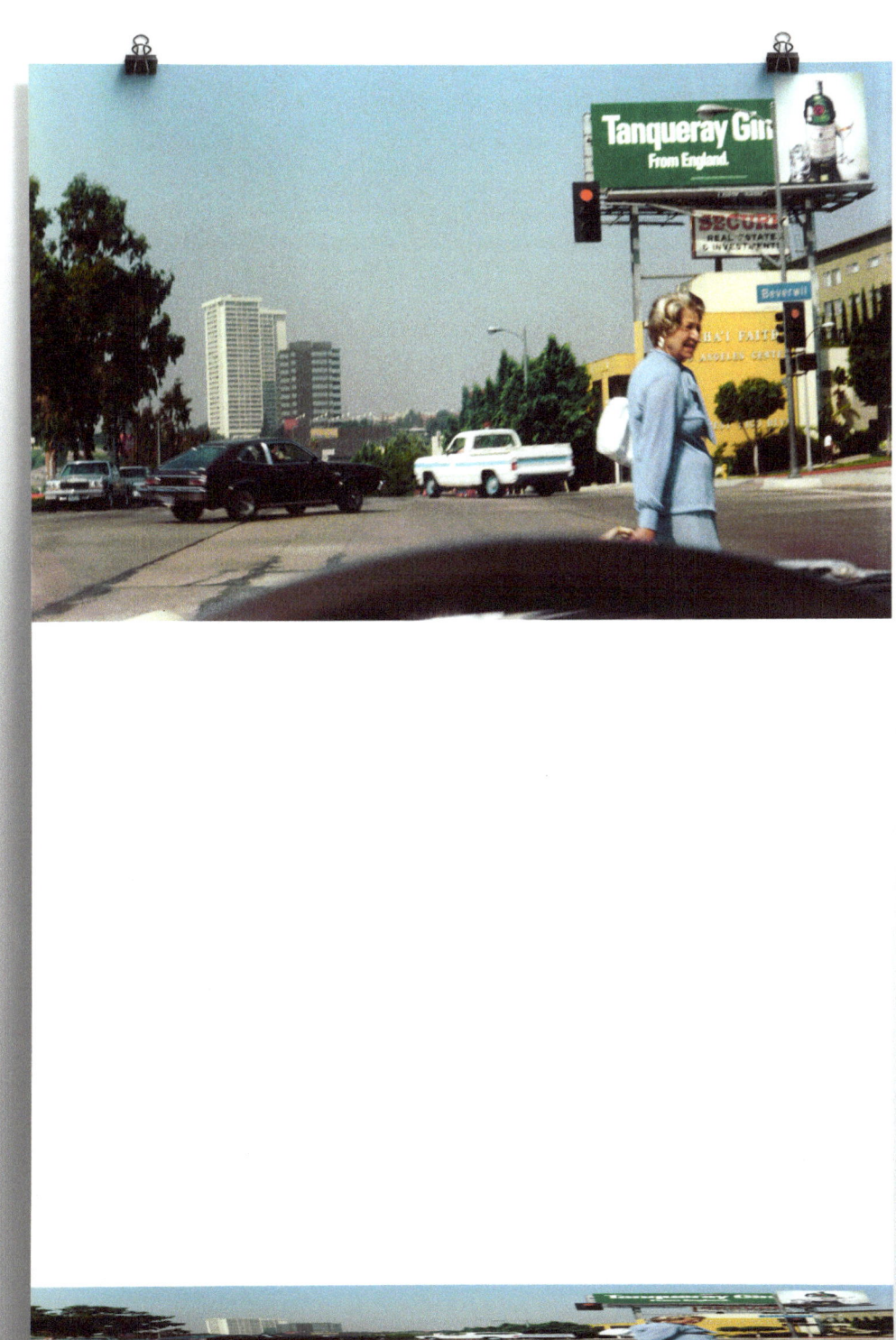

GFLA Olympic & Beverwil 1979
32 x 46 in

119

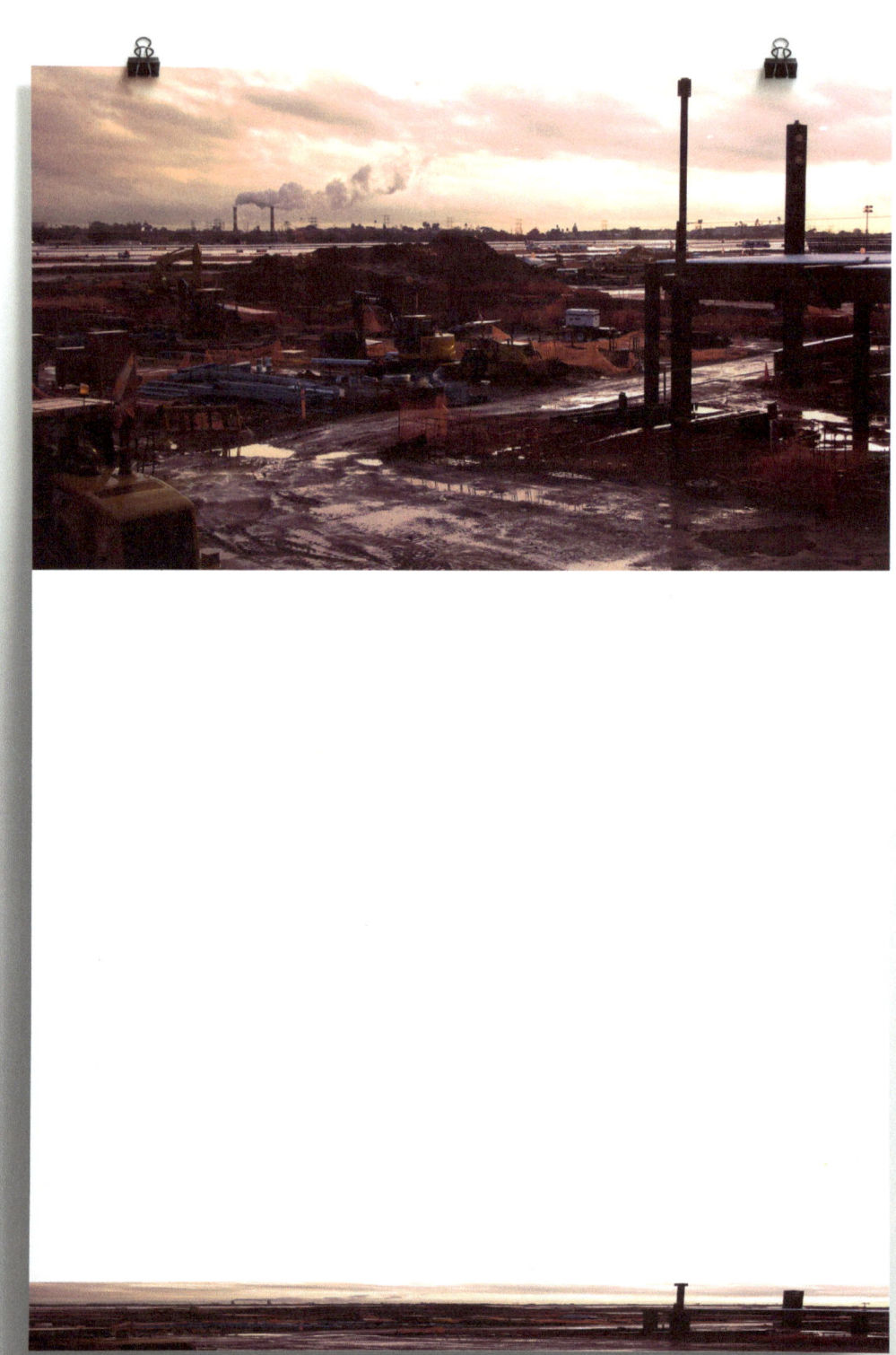

GFLA Inglewood 2011
32 x 46 in

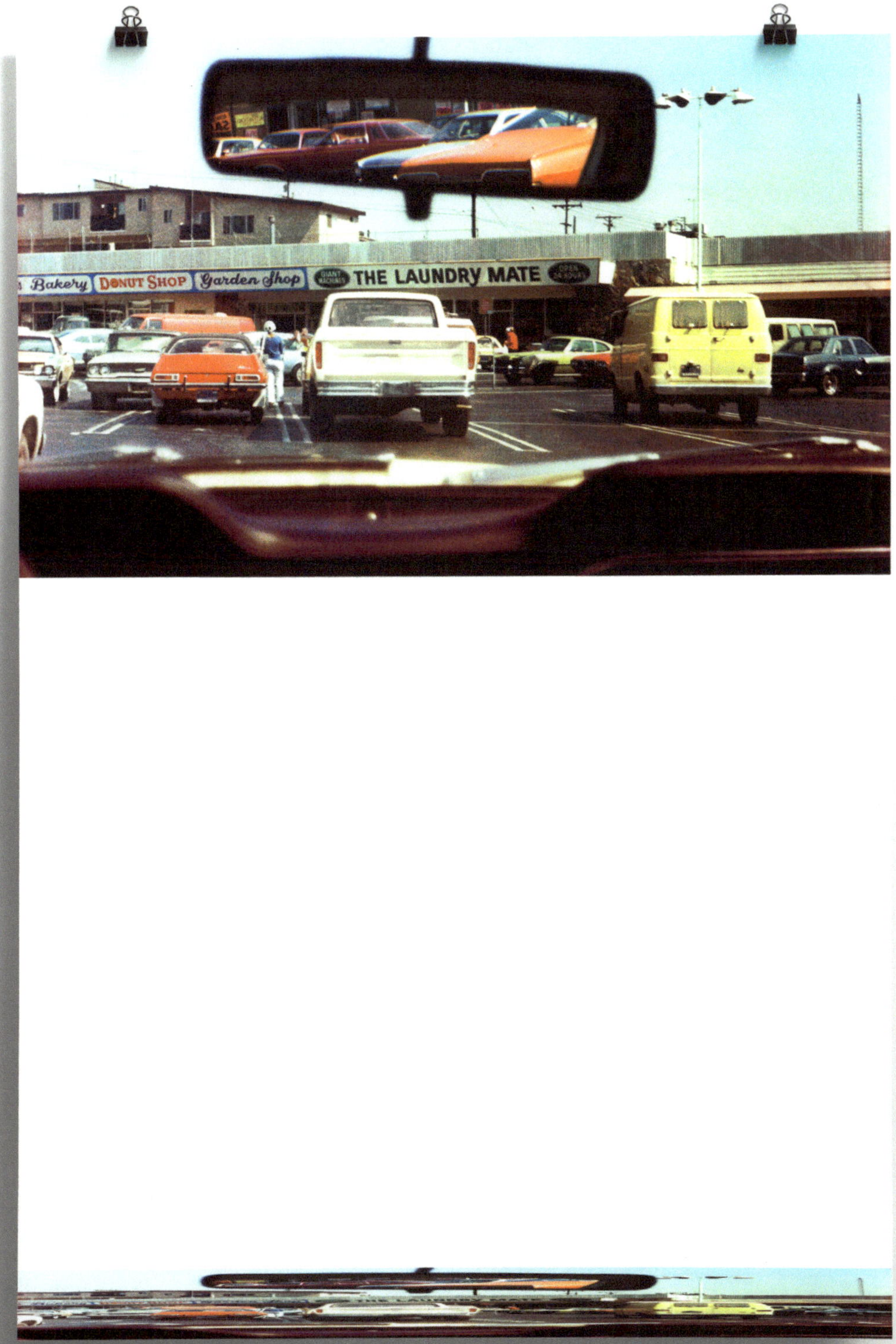

GFLA Hawthorne 1979
32 x 46 in

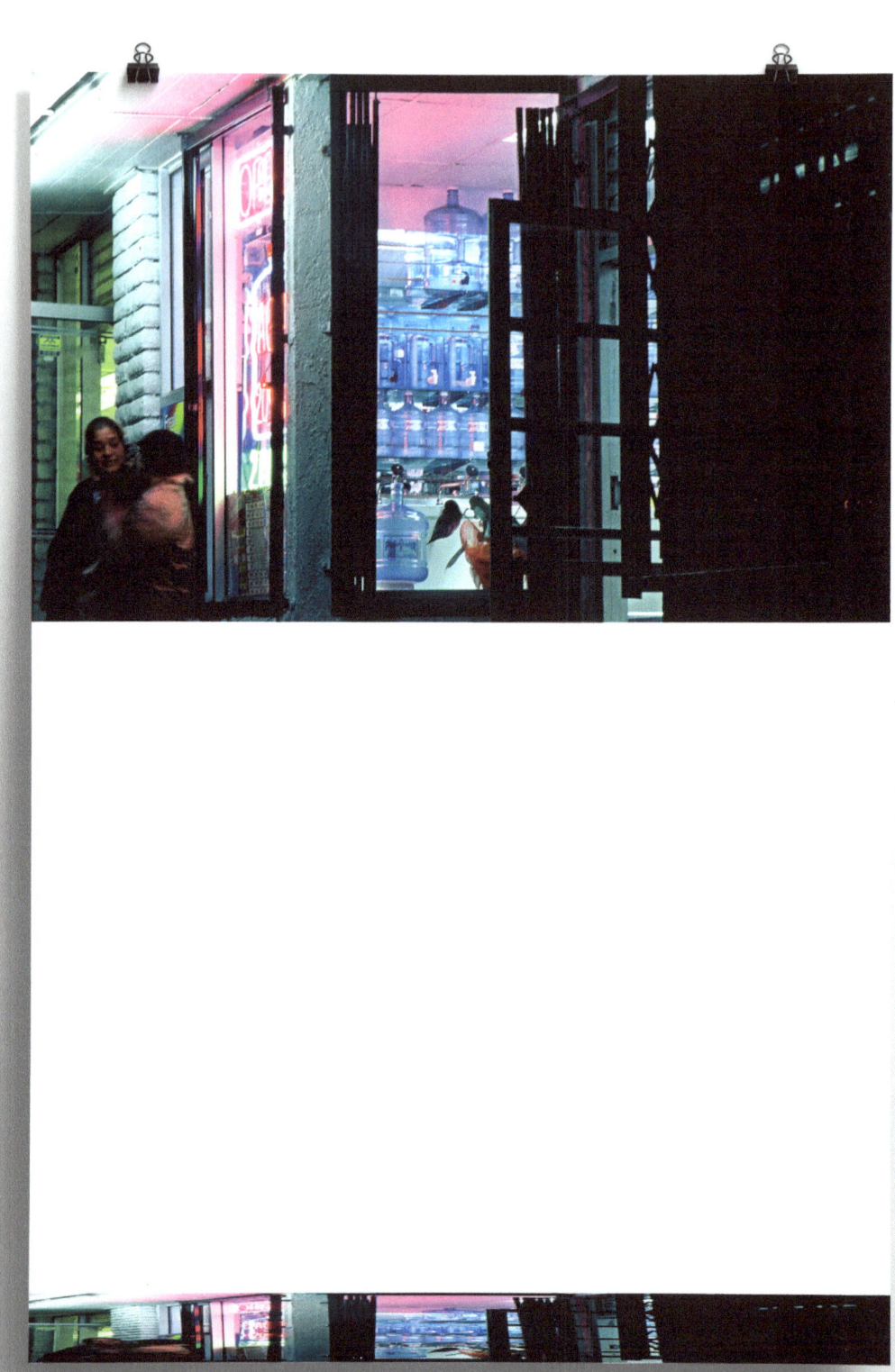

GFLA Echo Park 2004
32 x 46 in

122

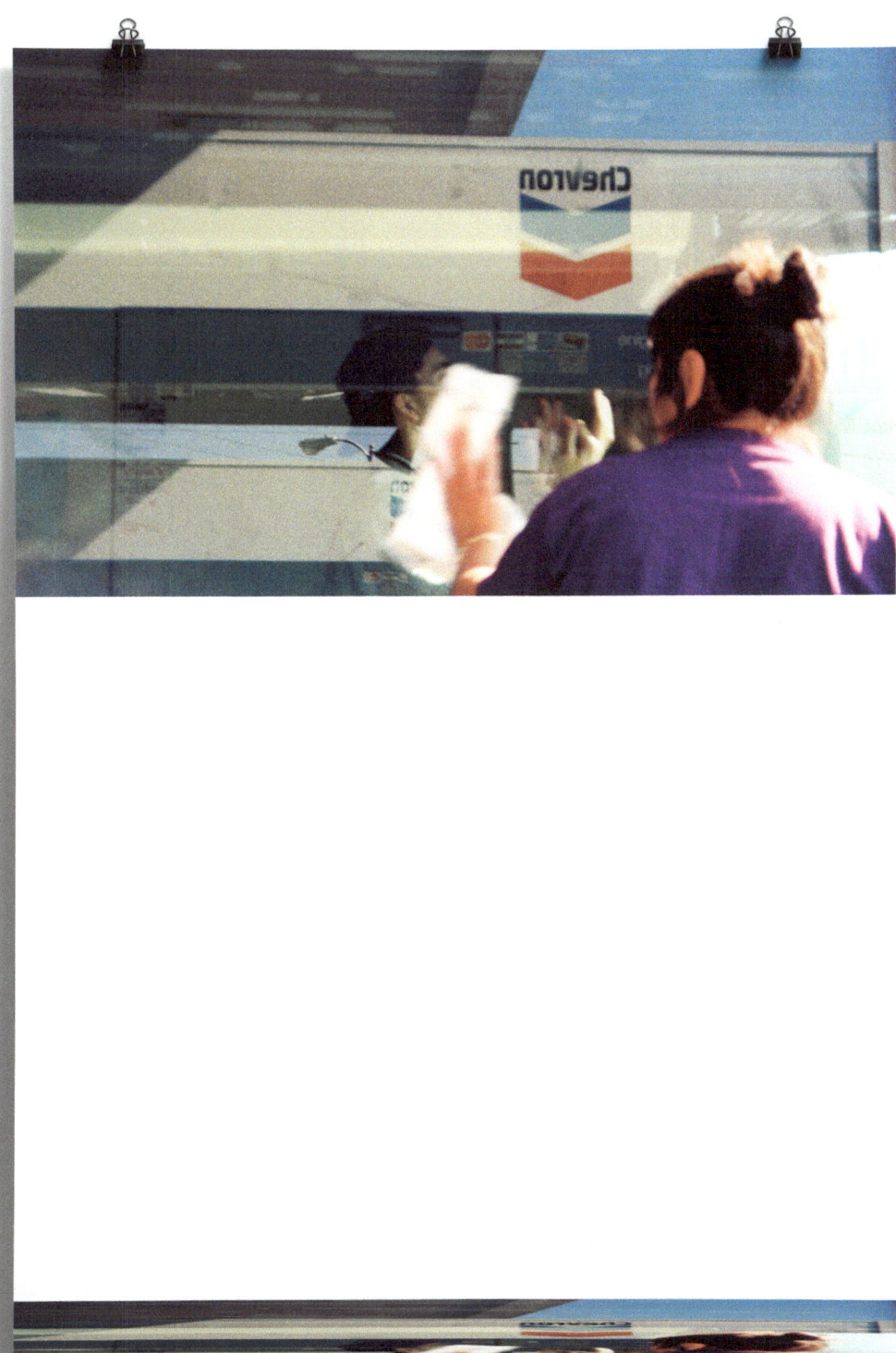

GFLA Pasadena 2001
32 x 46 in

123

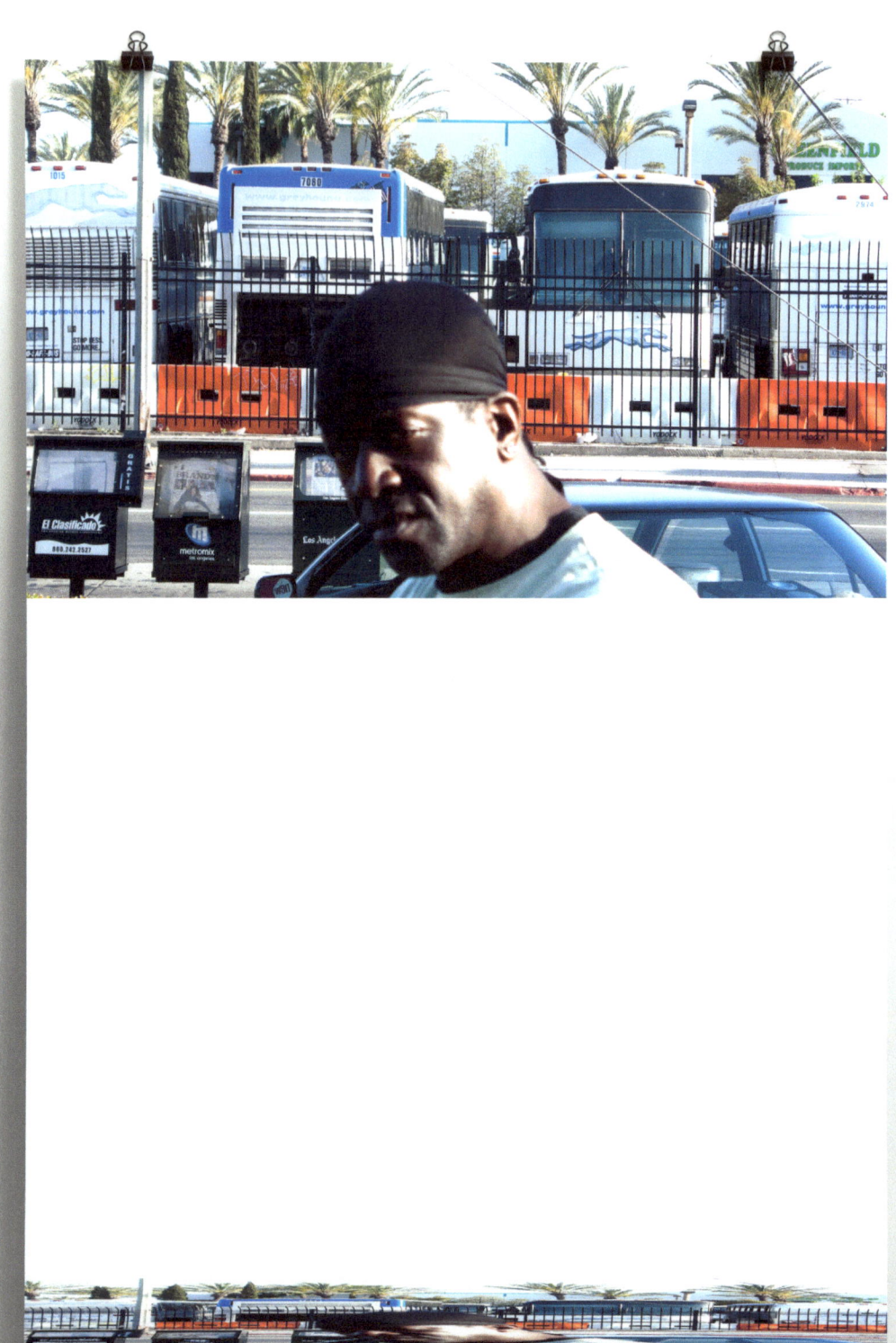

GFLA Alameda & 7th 2012
32 x 46 in

GFLA Atwater 2012
32 x 46 in

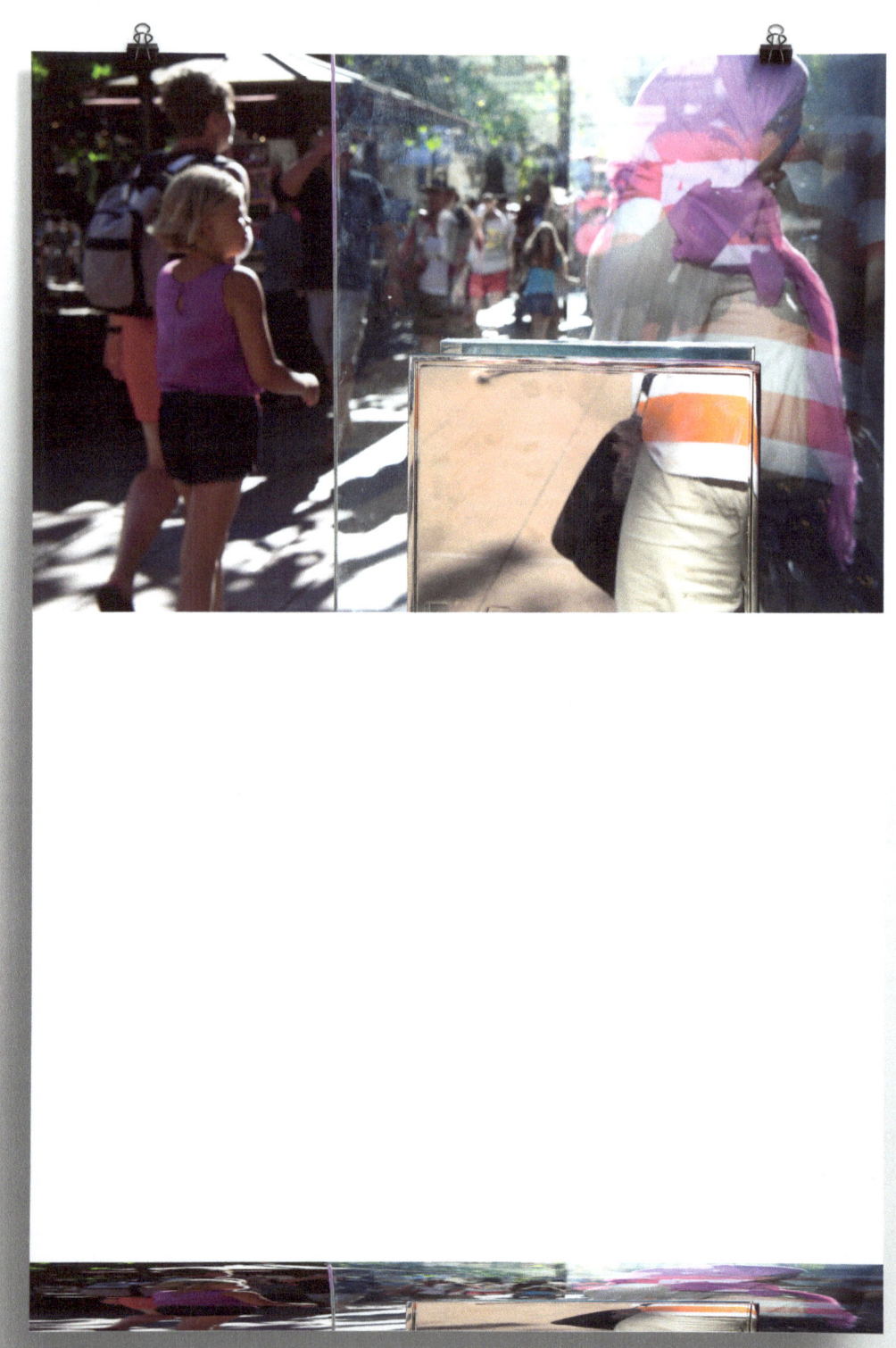

GFLA Beverly Grove 2010
32 x 46 in

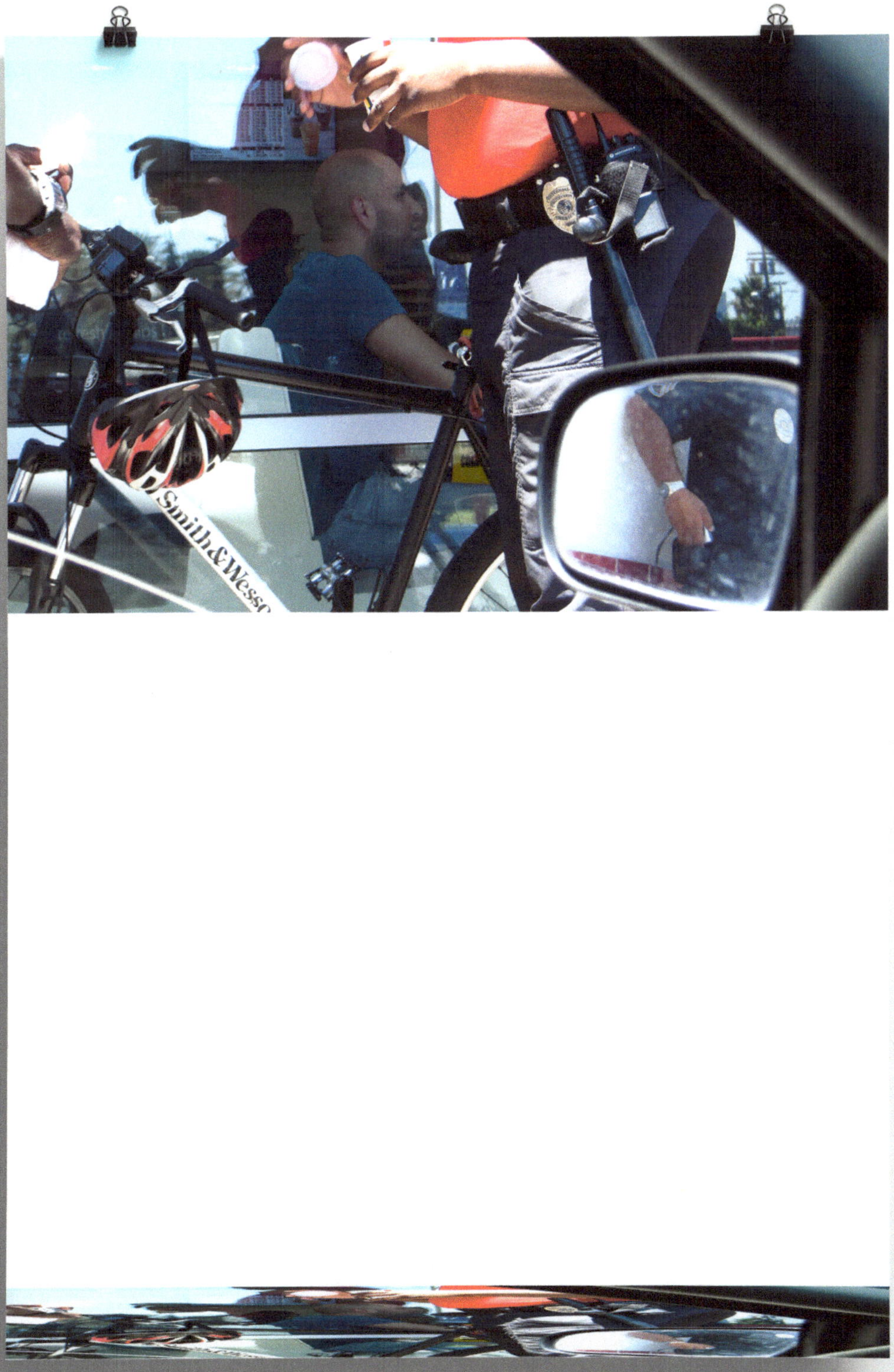

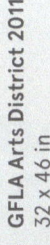

GFLA Arts District 2011
32 x 46 in

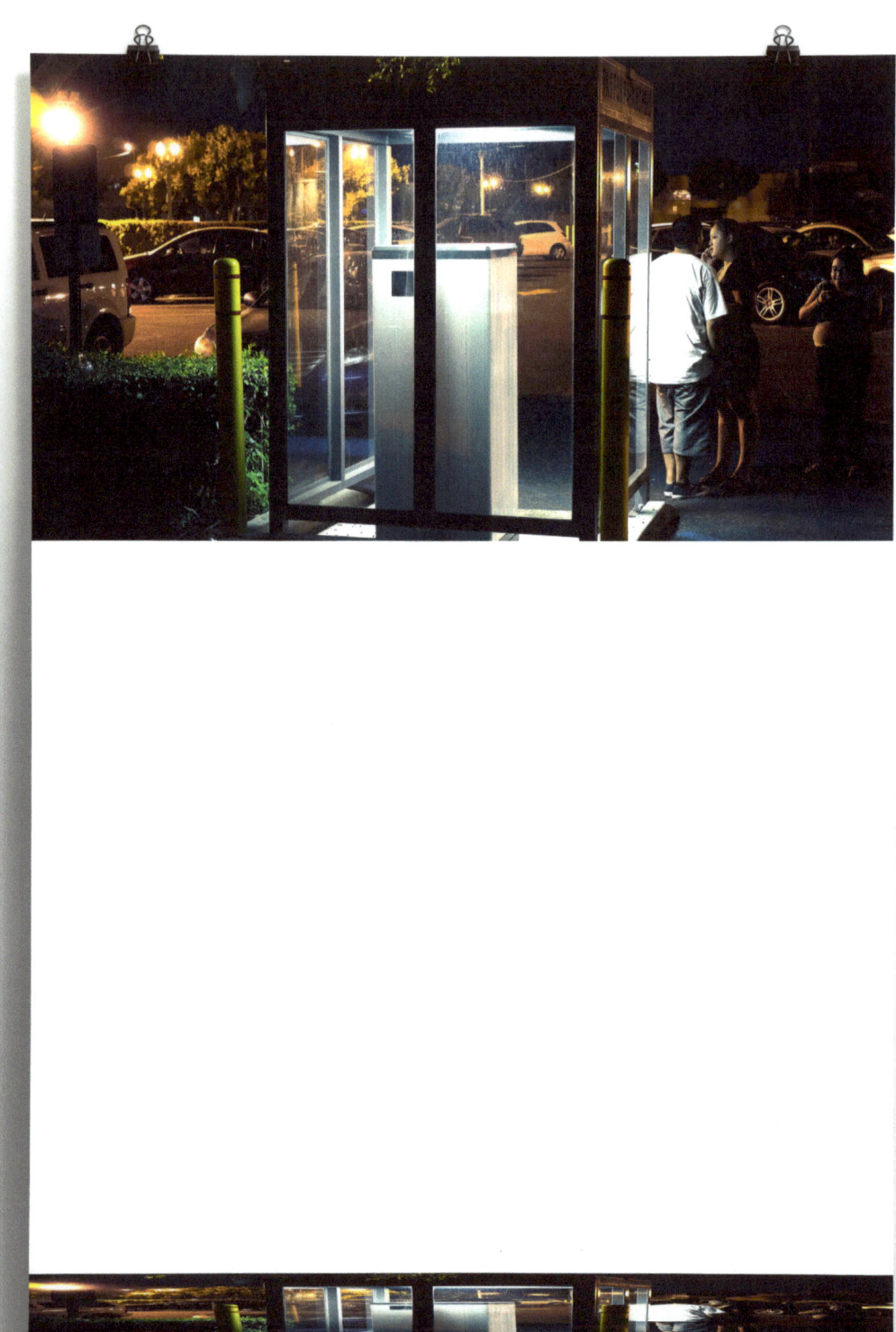

GFLA Broadway & Washington Blvd 2014
32 x 46 in

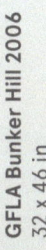

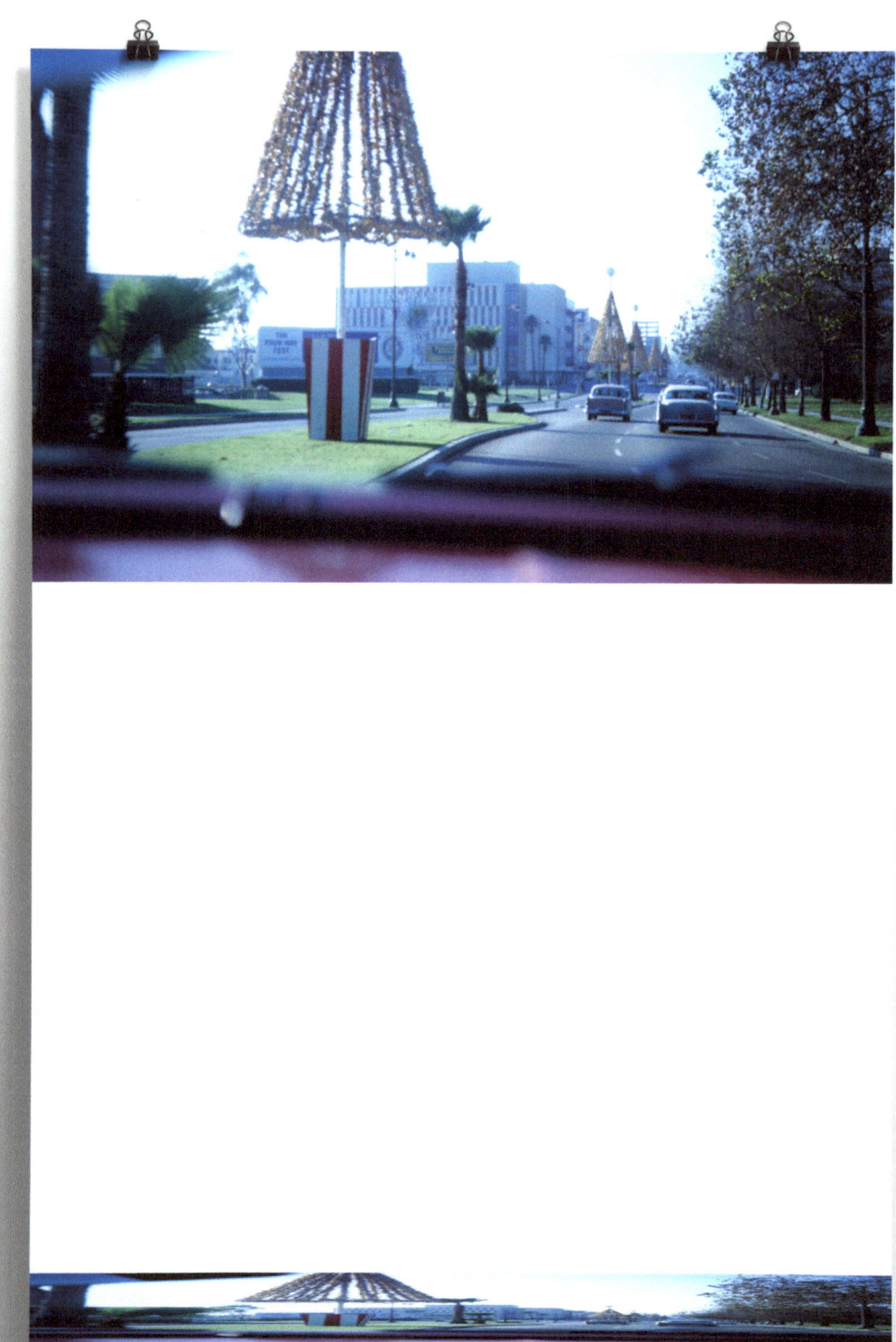

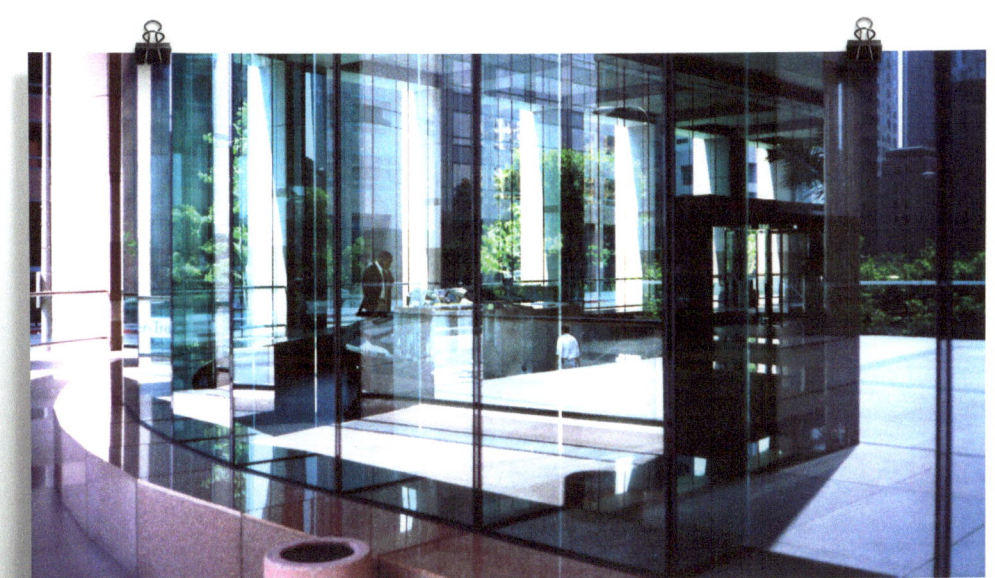

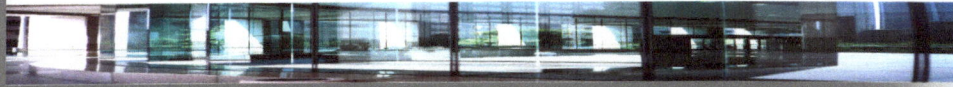

GFLA California Plaza 2001
32 x 46 in

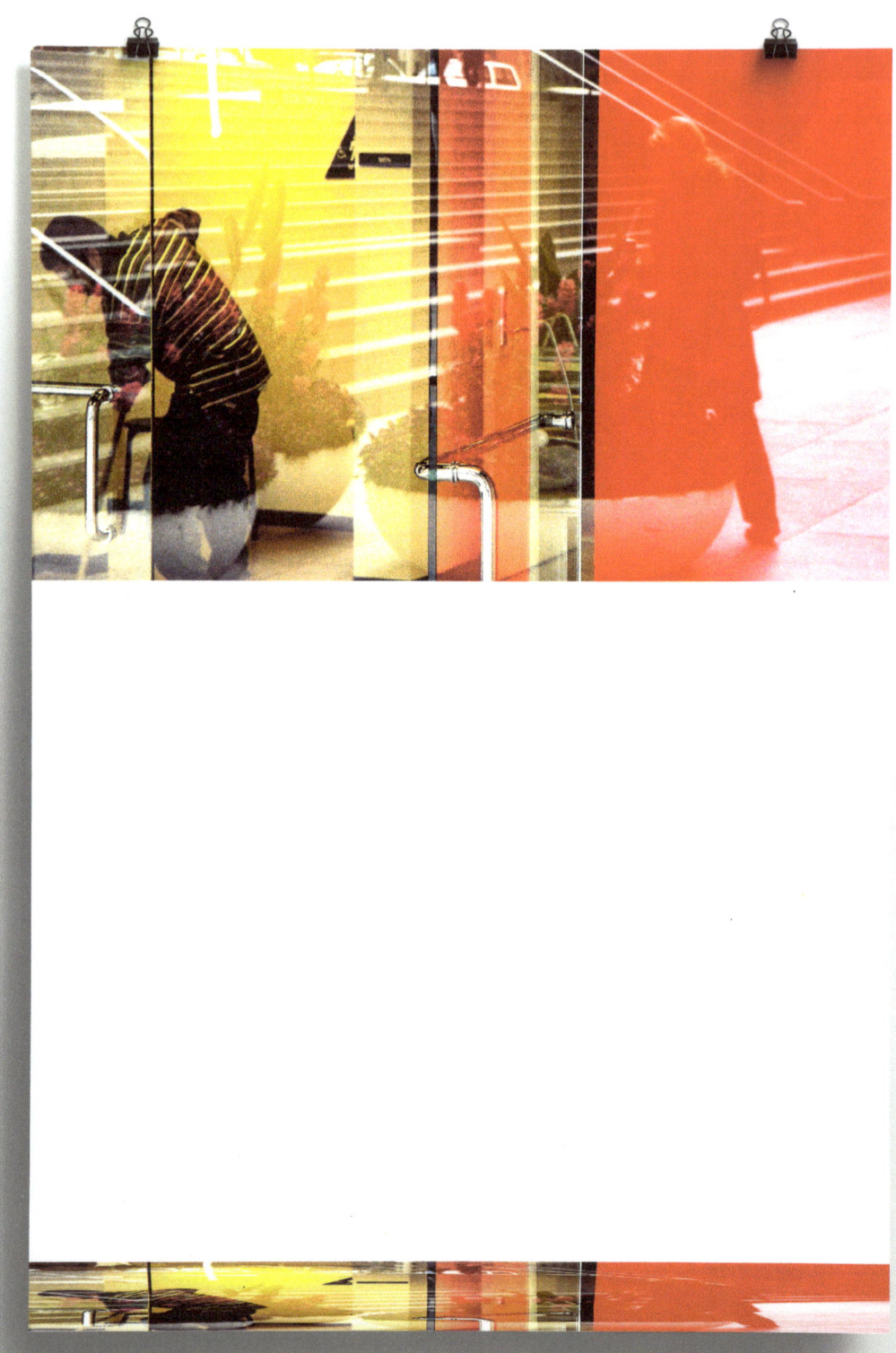

GFLA Civic Center 2006
32 x 46 in

132

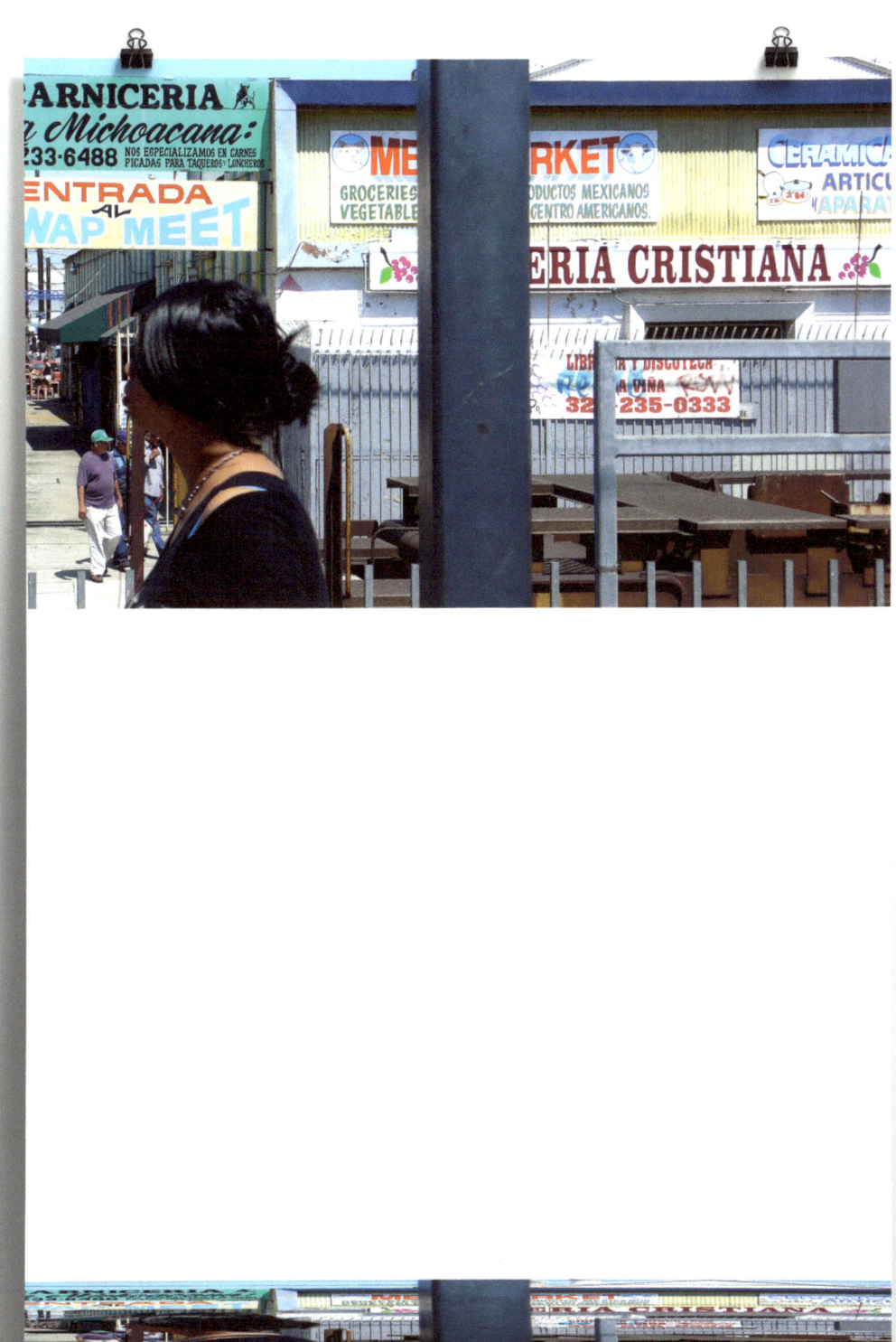

George Porcari

Born: 1952 Lima, Peru
Emigrated to Los Angeles 1963
Moved to New York City 1979
Returned to Los Angeles 1984

Education

Pratt Institute
Brooklyn, New York

Art Center College of Design
Pasadena, California

Exhibitions

Haphazard Gallery
Greetings From LA: 24 Frames and 50 Years
January 2016

Tif's Desk at Thomas Solomon's Gallery
Insistent Particularities
October 2012

China Art Objects
Just Everyday Matters: an Exhibition of Photographs 1963-2009
March 2010

Momenta Gallery
Untreated Strangeness, Group Show
Curator: Chris Kraus with Jorge Pardo
and Naomi Fisher
Brooklyn, New York
October 2009

China Art Objects
10 Year Anniversary Show, Group exhibition
Los Angeles, California
April 2009

Automat
I (Heart) Oregonia, With Tif Sigfrids
Los Angeles, California
November 2008

Mandarin Gallery
I See Through You, One person exhibition
Los Angeles, California
June 2006

Mandarin Gallery
Greetings From LA 1979!, One person exhibition
June 2006

China Art Objects
Shape Shifters, Group exhibition
Los Angeles, California
November 2005

Mandarin Gallery
Memory Verite, Two person exhibition with Miriam Noske
January 2005
Los Angeles, California

China Art Objects
Two person exhibition with Sharon Lockhart
Los Angeles, California
April 1999

Shoshana Wayne Gallery
Limeños, One person exhibition
Santa Monica, California
March 1999

Charim Klocker Gallery
Group exhibition
Vienna, Austria
May 1998

Shoshana Wayne Gallery
One person exhibition
Santa Monica, California
January 1998

Skirball Museum
New Beginnings, Group exhibition
Los Angeles, California
January 1997

Los Angeles County Museum of Art
P.L.A.N. (Photography in Los Angeles Now)
Group exhibition
Los Angeles, California
February 1996

Long Beach Museum of Art
Love in the Ruins, Group exhibition
Long Beach, California
November 1994

Bradbury Building
The Bradbury Building Show, Group exhibition
Los Angeles California
Summer 1990

Laurie Rubin Gallery
One person exhibition
New York City
December 1988

Published Work by G. Porcari

<u>The Arc of a Dive</u>: The Photography of
Alexander Rodchenko and Leni Riefenstahl
CineAction, Spring 2015

<u>Doubting Thomas</u>: Photography and Antonioni's Blow-Up
CineAction, Summer 2013

<u>Nobody's Vision</u>: Jim Jarmusch's Dead Man
CineAction, Spring 2012

<u>Antonioni's Orgy</u>: Zabriskie Point
CineAction ,Summer 2011

<u>The Biggest Film Biographer in the World</u>:
The Films of Ken Russell for the BBC
CineAction, Spring 2010

<u>We the Undead</u>: Nadja
Cine Action, Spring 2009

<u>Fellini Goes to the Beach</u>
CineAction, Summer 2008

<u>Fellini's Forgotten Masterpiece</u>: Toby Dammit
CineAction, Spring 2007

<u>Marriage and Its Discontents</u>: Torpor by Chris Kraus
Rain-Taxi, September/October 2006

A Bridge in Blythe and a Vortex in Time:
the Novels of W.G. Sebald
NY Arts, March/April 2005

Playing Out the Photography of Concern:
Starbucks Coffee in LA, Sharon Lockhart's Teatro
Amazonas in Brazil and Werner Bischoff in Lima, Peru
NY Arts, May/June 2004

Valerie Jouve: Concrete Poetry
Soma magazine, December/January 2002

Interview With Wong Kar-Wai
Soma magazine, January 2001

I Was an Artist for the 20th Century
Soma magazine, September 2000

Fellini's Ocean and Mariko's Dance
Inflatable Magazine, Fall 2000

The Photographer of Modern Life: Some Thoughts on
Sharon Lockhart's Untitled
Inflatable Magazine, Fall 1998

Western Sighs: The Doom Generation and Lost Highway
Inflatable Magazine, Spring 1997

Richard Prince
Arts Magazine, May 1987

Publications About G. Porcari

The Aesthetic of Reappearance
by Sylvére Lotringer
published by Tif's Desk 2012

Untreated Strangeness
by Chris Kraus
From *Where Art Belongs,* Semiotext(e) 2011

El Laberinto
by Mark von Schlegell
Untreated Strangeness Catalog published by
Momenta Art 2009

Shadows, Catastrophe, Happiness
by Sylvére Lotringer
Untreated Strangeness Catalog published by
Momenta Art 2009

Undesirable Alien
by Veronica Gonzalez
Untreated Strangeness Catalog published by
Momenta Art 2009

Untreated Strangeness at Momenta Art
by Holland Cotter
New York Times, December 4th, 2009

Pictures by Porcari
by Chris Kraus
C: International, Winter 2006

Now and Then
by Veronica Gonzalez
Mandarin Gallery 2006

George Porcari

Porcari at Shoshana Wayne
by Charlene Roth
New Art Examiner, July/August 1999

Porcari at Shoshana Wayne
by David Pagel
Los Angeles Times, January 1998

Bliss
L.A.C.E. 1997

New Beginnings
Skirball Museum 1996

Love in the Ruins
by Denise Spampinato
Long Beach Museum of Art 1994

Playing With the Truth
by Jeremy Gilbert-Rolfe
Laurie Rubin Gallery 1988

Films

Greetings From L.A. 1978!
6 minutes, 1978
A Super-8 film about various part of the city of Los Angeles with which I was familiar—made a few months before moving to New York City.

The Night Crew
(made with Doug Lee)
30 minutes, 1989, Betamax, Hi-8
A film about the Mexican immigrants who every evening clean the modernist landmark building by Craig Ellwood: The Art Center College of Design in Pasadena.

The House of Fiction
30 minutes, 1987–2000, Betamax, High-8, Digital Video
A film about the closing of the oldest surviving bookstore in Pasadena: The House of Fiction and a biography of its owner Bill Tunilla. The film also chronicles my failed attempt to make a conventional narrative film with a young woman in the same location in 1987.

David at China
15 minutes, 2001, Digital Video
A film about the posthumous exhibit of the artist David Von Schlagell at China Art Objects Gallery in Los Angeles. The film chronicles the exhibit, organized by his son Mark along with Steve Hanson and Giovanni Intra from hanging to opening night.

Wedding in Death Valley
13 minutes, 2003, Digital Video
The wedding of two friends in Death Valley California, near Zabriskie Point is documented.

With Glenn Gould
30 minutes, 2005
A Collage film made from appropriated footage about the young Glenn Gould's trip to New York in 1957 to record Bach's Italian Concerto.

The Beauty and the Beast
(dedicated to Chris Marker)
30 minutes, 2006
A collage film made from appropriated footage. The film is a re-telling of the legend transformed into a narrative about a visitor from a post-apocalyptic future who returns to the past (1962) in order to set things right.

Magic Gas
30 minutes, 2007, Digital Video
A document of a folk/rock concert held in a gas station in Echo Park in Los Angeles named Magic Gas.

Tif and Tom Play the Unknown
4 minutes, 2008, Digital Video
Documents a concert performance by Tif Sigfrids and Tom Watson of Neil Young's Mr. Soul at a club in Hollywood called "The Unknown".

15 Jokes Told by 15 Artists in 15 Minutes
(made with Tif Sigfrids)
15 minutes, 2008, Digital Video
Documents a performance by Tif Sigfrids in which she assigns jokes written by her to 15 artists during an opening of their work at Circus Gallery in Los Angeles. Things do not go as planned.

I (Heart) Oregonia
(made with Tif Sigfrids)
30 minutes, 2008, Digital Video
A film about a trip back home for Tif Sigfrids—to Oregonia Ohio—where she meets up with her family and friends for sing-a-longs and talks around the kitchen ending in a birthday trip to the Little River Café for a night of drinking and Karaoke.

A Parallel
30 minutes, 2010, Digital video
Made from appropriated footage. An astronaut's mission in 1963 goes horribly wrong as he returns to earth and begins to experience recent history in a loop from which there seems to be no escape.

Eileen Myles at China Art Objects
20 minutes, 2010, Digital video
Eileen Myles reads from her collection of essays The Importance of being Iceland: Travel Essays in Art.

Waiting For Brainard
(in collaboration with Tif Sigfrids)
25 minutes, 2011, Digital video
An adaption of Eric Rohmer's short film The Bakery Girl of Monceau set in contemporary Echo Park, a suburb of Los Angeles.

Sol With Cloud
(in collaboration with Tif Sigfrids and Colin Blodorn)
3 minutes, Digital Video
A baby is left alone for three minutes in an art gallery while a cloud wanders in.

Notes

Introduction

1   Walter Benjamin. "Little History of Photography." *The Work of Art in the Age of its Technological Reproducibility and Other Writings on Media.* Harvard University Press, 2008.

2   Walter Benjamin. "This Space For Rent." *One-Way Street, and Other Writings.* NLB, 1979.

3   Walter Benjamin. *Illuminations.* Harcourt, Brace & World, 1968.

4   Walter Benjamin, Rolf Tiedemann. *The Arcades Project.* Belknap Press, 1999.

5   Walter Benjamin, Michael William Jennings. "Little History of Photography." *Walter Benjamin: Selected Writings, Volume 2.* Belknap, 2005

6   Walter Benjamin, Michael William Jennings. "Little History of Photography." *Walter Benjamin: Selected Writings, Volume 2.* Belknap, 2005

Photographic Adventures with Edgar Degas

1   Hofmann, Werner. *Degas: A Dialogue of Difference.* Thames and Hudson, 2007.

2   Hofmann, Werner. *Degas: A Dialogue of Difference.* Thames and Hudson, 2007.

3   Heilbrun, Francoise. *Musee d'Orsay: Photography.* Scala, France, 2006.

4   Clark, Kenneth. *The Nude.* Princeton University Press, 1972.

5   Hambourg, Maria Morris. *Nadar.* Metropolitan Museum of Art, 1995.

New Palimpsests From the Zen Arcade

1   Steiner, George. *The Poetry of Thought: From Hellenism to Celan.* 158.

2   Benjamin, Walter. *The Arcades Project.* 456.

The Delight of the Particular:
Photographs by Ronald Traeger

1   Barthes, Roland. "The Photographic Message." *The Responsibility of Forms: Critical Essays on Music, Art, and Representation*, 1985.

2   Martin Harrison, Tessa Traeger. *Ronald Traeger: New Angles.* Schirmer/Mosel, 1999.

3   Martin Harrison, Jonathan Cape. *Young Meteors: British Photojournalism: 1957–1965*, 1998.

4   Martin Harrison, Jonathan Cape. *Young Meteors: British Photojournalism: 1957–1965*, 1998.

www.ingramcontent.com/pod-product-compliance
Lightning Source LLC
Chambersburg PA
CBHW041313180526
45172CB00004B/1078